Everyman's Poetry

*Everyman, I will go with thee,
and be thy guide*

Homer

Selected verse from
the *Iliad* and the *Odyssey*

Translated by ALEXANDER POPE

Edited by DAVID HOPKINS
University of Bristol

EVERYMAN
J. M. Dent · London

This edition first published by Everyman Paperbacks in 1999
Selection, introduction and other critical apparatus
© J.M. Dent 1999

J.M. Dent
Orion Publishing Group
Orion House
5 Upper Saint Martin's Lane
London WC2H 9EA

Typeset by Deltatype Ltd, Birkenhead, Merseyside
Printed in Great Britain by
The Guernsey Press Co. Ltd, Guernsey, C.I.

British Library Cataloguing-in-Publication
Data is available on request

ISBN 0 460 87997 9

Contents

from The Iliad

from The Odyssey

Note on the Author, Translator and Editor

'HOMER' was the name given in antiquity to the author of two epic poems, the *Iliad* and *Odyssey* – the earliest and most famous works of ancient Greek literature. Though he was believed to be an historical figure, nothing certain was known about his identity or life. One ancient tradition associated him with the island of Chios, where a guild of 'Homeridae', or 'reciters of Homer', existed from the sixth century BC. Another held that he was blind. The Homeric poems were revered throughout antiquity, and widely studied in Greek and Roman schools. After their rediscovery at the Renaissance, they once again acquired a high literary status, though a number of influential critics of the sixteenth, seventeenth, and eighteenth centuries judged them to be primitive, indecorous, immoral and ill-constructed. During the nineteenth and early twentieth centuries, interest shifted from the poems' literary qualities to their origins and historical background. Their standing as works of art was substantially modified by the developing belief that they were the products not of individual authorship, but of a tradition of oral improvisation, in which stock themes, techniques and phrasing were shared and redeployed by a succession of anonymous 'bards'. Recent scholarship, however, has revived the older notion of an individual 'Homer' – or, more commonly, two 'Homers', each with a rather different artistic temperament and priorities: an '*Iliad* poet', whose awesome epic of heroic warfare and human suffering dates from 750–700 BC, and a slightly later '*Odyssey* poet', whose less stringent imaginings focus on adventure, enchantment, the pleasures of family and community, and the justice of the gods.

ALEXANDER POPE (1688–1744) is best known today as a satirist, but it was his translation of Homer (*Iliad*, 1715–20; *Odyssey*, with collaborators, 1725–6) which made his fortune and fame. Pope's *Iliad* is a sustained celebration of the 'invention', 'fire', 'rapture' and 'commanding impetuosity' which he found in his original. It was described by Samuel Johnson as a 'poetical wonder . . . which no age or nation can pretend to equal'. In our own day, is has been described as 'arguably the finest English poem in heroic couplets' (Martin Mueller) and as 'a masterpiece in its own right, and an epic which, as far as English goes, comes second only to Milton' (George Steiner).

DAVID HOPKINS read Classics and English at St Catharine's College, Cambridge, and is currently Reader in English Poetry at the University of Bristol. He is the editor of *Dryden* and *Ovid* in the 'Everyman's Poetry' series. His publications have mainly been concerned with English poetry of the seventeenth and eighteenth centuries, and with English/Classical literary relations.

Chronology: the Homeric epics and their afterlife

Year	Event
c. 1600–1100 BC	'Mycenaean' civilization: a literate, Greek-speaking, bureaucratic palace culture centring on great fortified citadels (Mycenae, Tiryns, Pylos, Thebes); some place-names, verbal forms and artefacts from this period (e.g. bronze weapons) preserved as fossilized memories in the Homeric epics.
c. 1270 BC	Destruction of 'Troy VI', a layer of the bronze age citadel in Asia Minor (at Hissarlik in modern Turkey), identified by some scholars with the 'Troy' of the Homeric poems.
c. 1190 BC	Destruction of 'Troy VIIa', also at Hissarlik, another possible candidate for Homer's city.
c. 1100 BC	General destruction of Mycenaean civilization by Dorian invasions from the north, leading to the so-called Dark Age; loss of literacy in Greece.
c. 850 BC	Reintroduction of writing into Greece, using an adapted form of the Phoenician alphabet.
776 BC	Traditional date for the introduction of the Olympian Games, an early expression of a new-found pan-Hellenic consciousness.
c. 750–700 BC	Probable date of the *Iliad*, the earliest extant work of Greek literature.
c. 725–675 BC	Probable date of the *Odyssey*; both poems attributed by most ancient sources to a single poet, 'Homer', along with a number of other heroic epics on the Trojan saga; some circumstantial details and social assumptions of the poems (e.g. iron tools, cremation) similar to those of the late-Dark-Age world in which they were composed.

Year	Event
6thC BC	*Iliad* and *Odyssey* differentiated at around this time from the other heroic epics; legislation introduced at Athens to ensure complete recitations of the *Iliad* and *Odyssey* at the Panathenaea; some linguistic features of both poems probably revised for the benefit of Athenian audiences.
late 6thC BC onwards	A guild of 'Homeridae' ('reciters of Homer'), said to be Homer's descendants, flourishing on the island of Chios, often claimed as Homer's birthplace.
c. 525 BC	*Floruit* of the grammarian and critic Theagenes of Rhegium, purportedly the first of many scholars to offer allegorical readings of Homer (with the 'strife' of the gods being equated with the 'strife' of the elements, etc.).
384–322 BC	Lifetime of Aristotle, whose *Poetics* stressed the unity of the Homeric poems.
3rd–2ndCs BC	Establishment of the 'standard' text of Homer by the Alexandrian scholars Zenodotus (b. *c.* 325 BC), Aristophanes of Byzantium (*c.* 257–180 BC), and Aristarchus (*c.* 216–144 BC); the texts of the epics scrutinized, suspect lines rejected or emended, explanatory 'scholia' (annotations) appended, and the epics divided into twenty-four books each.
30 BC	Arrival at Rome of the Greek rhetorician, Dionysius of Halicarnassus, whose *On Literary Composition* contains telling praise of Homer's capacity to make charming poetry out of the simplest and most everyday incidents and the plainest language.
29–19 BC	Composition of the *Aeneid*, Virgil's epic on the legend of Aeneas and the foundation of Rome, heavily and continuously influenced by the Homeric poems.
?1stC AD	Composition of the treatise *On the Sublime* by 'Longinus', containing famous and influential

Year	Event
	praise of the 'sublime' grandeur and drama of the *Iliad*, and the combination of romantic fable and domestic realism in the *Odyssey*.
earlier than AD 68	Composition of the *Ilias Latina*, a Latin epitome of the *Iliad*; together with the Trojan narratives of 'Dares of Phrygia' (5th/6thC AD) and 'Dictys of Crete' (4thC AD), a main source of Homeric material in Western Europe during the Greekless Middle Ages.
3rdC AD	Celebrated allegorical interpretation of Homer by the scholar and philosopher Porphyry (AD 234–*c.* 305).
12thC AD	Compilation of a vast explanatory commentary on Homer (drawing on earlier Greek material) by Eustathius, Bishop of Thessalonica.
1488	Publication of the first printed edition of Homer in Florence, edited by Chalcondyles of Athens, an immigrant teacher of Greek in Italy; first-hand knowledge of Homer, however, remained scanty, and the epics were chiefly read with the aid of (often inadequate) Latin translations.
1561	Celebrated attack on Homer in *Poetices Libri Septem* by the Italian humanist, Julius Caesar Scaliger, setting, along with the *Ars Poetica* of Marco Girolamo Vida (*c.* 1489–1566), the tone for much continental discussion of the two poets during the sixteenth, seventeenth, and early eighteenth centuries: Homer seen as prolix and indecorous, his imagery as unpalatably homely, his treatment of the gods as irreverent, and his heroes as murderous and barbaric; Virgil's greater decorum, and emphasis on civic duty and imperial destiny, generally preferred.
1598–1611	Publication of George Chapman's translation of the *Iliad* in 'fourteeners' (praised by Keats in a famous sonnet).

Year	Event
1614	Publication of Chapman's *Odyssey* in iambic pentameter couplets.
1667	First edition of Milton's *Paradise Lost*, the principal English epic; the blind Milton seeing himself, in important respects, as an 'English Homer'.
1674	Publication of Boileau's influential French translation of Longinus' *On the Sublime*.
1692	Publication of the Volume 3 of Charles Perrault's *Parallèle des anciens et des modernes*, reviving many of the Renaissance criticisms of Homer.
1699	Publication of *Télémaque* by François de Salignac de la Mothe-Fénelon (1651–1715), a moralizing pedagogical romance, retelling the 'missing' adventures of Telemachus between Book 4 and Book 15 of the *Odyssey*.
1711	Influential edition and French translation of Homer by Mme Dacier (1672–1731), emphasizing the need for an historical understanding of Homer's age and literary assumptions.
1715–20	Publication of Alexander Pope's translation of the *Iliad*, the most widely admired and frequently reprinted version in English.
1725–26	Publication of Pope's *Odyssey* (with the collaboration of William Broome and Elijah Fenton).
1727	Publication of Voltaire's *Essay on Epic Poetry*; Homer treated as a remote and primitive figure, of little interest in the modern world.
1730	Publication of *The Second New Science*, by the Italian philosopher, Giambattista Vico (1668–1744), including an essay 'On the Discovery of the True Homer'; the Homeric epics seen as folk poetry, embodying the manner of thinking of a whole community; some of Vico's ideas paralleled in the 'primitivist' criticism of the 1750s to 1780s,

Year	Event
	in which Homer is praised for manifesting the simplicity, wildness, sublimity and uncultivated genius characteristic of 'primitive' bards.
1767	Publication of Robert Wood's *Comparative View of the Ancient and Present State of the Troad, to which is prefixed an Essay on the Original Genius of Homer* (revised 1769, 1775); Homer praised for his accurate representations of the landscapes around Troy; Wood's volume an important influence on Goethe.
1791	Publication of William Cowper's translation of Homer, in Miltonic blank verse.
1795	Publication of F.A. Wolf's *Prolegomena to Homer*; the Homeric poems seen not as the work of a single poet but as compilations (via a prolonged, collaborative process) of pre-existing orally-recited poems; the beginning of so-called 'analytical' criticism of Homer.
1861	Publication of Matthew Arnold's lectures *On Translating Homer*; Arnold attempting to define the 'general effect' of Homer's epics, and to judge how far this had been captured by Homer's English translators.
1870–1890	Excavation by the German archaeologist Heinrich Schliemann (1822–90) of the mound at Hissarlik, first identified as the site of Troy by Charles Maclaren in 1820.
1922	Publication of James Joyce's *Ulysses*, each incident of which has its counterpart in the *Odyssey*.
1928–37	Publication of influential studies by the American scholar, Milman Parry (1902–35), demonstrating that certain stylistic features of the Homeric poems (stock epithets, repeated scenes, etc.) derive from the techniques of improvised oral verse-making.

Year	Event
1940–1	Publication of 'The *Iliad* or the poem of force', an influential essay by the French philosopher Simone Weil (1909–43); Homer's world portrayed as one in which everything is subject to pitiless force, and retributive nemesis.
1947	Publication of E.V. Rieu's *Odyssey*, a modern prose rendering, as the first volume in the 'Penguin Classics' series (Rieu's *Iliad*, 1950); over 3 million copies sold to date.
1951	Translation of the *Iliad* by Richmond Lattimore in loose six-beat lines; a line-for-line rendering of Homer's Greek; very influential through its widespread use in schools and universities (Lattimore's *Odyssey*, 1965).
1962	Free renderings of episodes from Homer by Christopher Logue (b. 1926) – *Patrocleia* (1962), *Pax* (1967), *GBH* (1981), *Kings* (1991), *The Husbands* (1994) – boldly incorporating modern allusions to 'make Homer new' for the late twentieth century.
1990	Publication of *Omeros* by Derek Walcott (1930–): Homeric incidents and characters freely drawn upon, in a tale of West Indian fishermen; Walcott's adaptation of The *Odyssey* performed by the Royal Shakespeare Company in 1992 (published 1993).

Introduction

The *Iliad* and *Odyssey*, the two epic poems ascribed in antiquity to 'Homer', are, in the view of most scholars, the earliest extant works of ancient Greek literature, and the earliest works of European poetry to be continuously remembered. Both are of great length (*Iliad* over 15,000 lines; *Odyssey* over 12,000). Both deploy an artificial 'poetic diction' which is remote from the spoken Greek of any particular time and place, and which combines a stylized formality with a direct plainness of expression. Both display features – repeated lines, formulaic phrases, stereotypical scenes – which are characteristic of orally-improvised verse. Both are set in an imaginary heroic past which, though some of its artefacts and customs are like those of Mycenaean or Dark-Age Greece, does not, as a whole, resemble any historical society. Both deploy the literary conventions which have become the stock-in-trade of the epic genre: invocations to the Muse, formal speeches, lengthy descriptions, interventions by the gods, 'long-tailed' similes. Both draw their plots from the saga of the Trojan War: the expedition mounted by a Greek army under the leadership of Agamemnon to recapture Helen, the wife of Agamemnon's brother, Menelaus, who had been abducted by Paris, the son of Priam, king of Troy.

The *Iliad*, a stark evocation of the glory, terror and pity of heroic warfare, is set in the tenth and final year of the Trojan War. It tells of the bitter quarrel between Agamemnon and Achilles, the mightiest and most passionate of the Greek warriors. Achilles withdraws from the fight, with disastrous consequences for the Greeks. But after the death of his best friend, Patroclus, at the hands of the Trojan prince, Hector, he is reconciled with Agamemnon, and returns to the battle, killing Hector in single combat. After dragging his opponent's corpse round the walls of Troy in full view of his parents, Achilles finally relents, abates his wrath, and returns Hector's body to Priam for cremation.

The less austere *Odyssey* – a more diverse and digressive narrative, with elements of adventure-story and magical romance, and a happy ending – tells of the voyage home from Troy of the wily and resourceful Greek warrior Ulysses (Odysseus). Having endured many hardships and perils, Ulysses finally reaches his homeland of Ithaca, where he takes his vengeance on the crowd of unruly suitors who have harassed his faithful wife, Penelope, during his twenty-year absence. Reunited with her, with his son Telemachus, and with his aged father Laertes, Ulysses restores peace and order to his kingdom.

Numerous questions have been asked about the background, provenance and substance of the Homeric poems: What is their date? Do their oral-improvisatory elements suggest that they were orally composed? Or were they fashioned with the aid of writing? Are they both the work of one hand? Or of two poets? Or of a succession of bards each making his anonymous contribution to a collaboratively evolving enterprise? How closely do the poems we read resemble those that were 'originally' composed by 'Homer'? How can one reconcile their clear and purposeful overall design with their local loose ends and inconsistencies? Was the Trojan War a 'real' event, or is it a pure fiction? Do the values, relationships and characters depicted in the Homeric poems strike immediately familiar chords with later readers, or do they seem bafflingly (or inspiringly) 'primitive' and 'alien'?

Many of these issues remain the object of controversy, though a broad consensus on a number of points has emerged. Most scholars now agree that, whatever elements of oral-improvisatory technique are deployed in the *Iliad* and *Odyssey*, the sophisticated shaping and co-ordination of both poems suggest individual authorship, rather than the cumulative efforts of a bardic 'team'. The *Iliad*, the current consensus suggests, was composed around 750–700 BC, with the *Odyssey* coming slightly later – probably the work of a second poet, well versed in his predecessor's work. Various interventions, the scholars concede, lie between us and the poems as 'originally' composed. Both epics, for example, were probably revised for the benefit of Athenian audiences in the sixth century, and both were certainly tidied by the Alexandrian scholars of the third and second centuries BC, when they were divided into the twenty-four book format in which we read them today. But uncertainties about the poems' origins and transmission, it is increasingly maintained, should not lead us to treat them as an aesthetic 'special case', fundamentally different in kind from the work of later European poets. There is no reason, most modern scholars suggest, why the literary qualities of 'Homer' should not be discussed in an essentially similar way to that in which one would discuss those of Shakespeare, Milton, or Pope.

The imaginative world of the Homeric poems, and particularly of the *Iliad*, is, nevertheless, one that has struck, and still strikes, many readers (particularly on first acquaintance) as uncomfortably archaic and barbaric. The *Iliad* depicts an aristocratic 'shame culture' operating according to strict codes of obligation, status, honour and fame, which, if breached, can provoke extremes of violence and destruction. Much of the glory and tragedy of the Homeric warrior's predicament is epitomized and concentrated in the figure of the *Iliad*'s hero, Achilles – by general consent the most awe-inspiring of the Greek warriors at Troy. Achilles has been told by his mother, the sea-nymph Thetis, that he is faced with a crucial life-choice: to fight at Troy, where he will die young but win immortal glory, or to stay at home, where he will live a long but undistinguished life. Achilles has chosen to fight, with a terrifyingly clear-sighted awareness of what his decision involves. He has come to Troy to achieve a glory that will be embodied, during the course of his short life, in the honour paid to him by his fellow warriors: hence his extreme sensitivity to any threats to his status. But he also knows that he will not survive to see the full extent of his fame, since that fame will be largely posthumous, and, for the Homeric warrior, the afterlife is a vague and shadowy prospect, offering little hope of consolation or repose. Everything, therefore, depends on how one deploys one's efforts in the short span that is allowed one, this side of the grave. For a while, after his quarrel with Agamemnon, Achilles reneges on his heroic choice and withdraws from battle. But after the death of Patroclus, he re-enters the fight, with an intensified realization that, whatever glory accrues to him from a victory over Hector, he will die at Troy.

Achilles has sometimes seemed an awkward protagonist, his vehement intransigence and violence corresponding less comfortably with readers' sense of what it means to be heroic than the tender humanity and resigned dutifulness of his adversary, Hector, or the pious patriotism of Virgil's Aeneas. And readers' unease with Achilles has often been extended to other aspects of the *Iliad*. Their discomfort has often led them to sanitize or censor Homer's text with allegorical or moralizing interpretations. The poem, however, constantly resists being straight-jacketed within any simple ethical frame of reference. Homer's sympathies are distributed with a remarkable flexibility, freedom and inclusiveness. He makes no simple discrimination, for example, between the rights and wrongs of the Greek and Trojan cases. He depicts the Trojan War as a site of heroic glory, but also as source of endless misery and unrest, in contrast with the peacetime world – of which we are constantly reminded in similes and digressions. He portrays the gods as immoral, devious and capricious, but also as majestically glorious. He shows us a Helen of Troy who is the cause of infinite suffering, but, simultaneously, a dignified victim of Venus's cruel attentions. He conveys with great pathos the plight of Priam, grieving over the loss of Hector, but simultaneously acknowledges that Achilles, too, is, in his own way, a fragile, suffering mortal.

Homer's style and manner have the same inclusiveness as his characters and conceptions, and encompass, sometimes in dizzyingly close proximity, the loftiest grandeur and the plainest simplicity. From the Renaissance onwards, one school of criticism has felt uneasy about the undignified bluntness with which Homer's heroes express themselves, and the plain-spoken, homely diction which the poet deploys in many of his similes and analogies. For commentators in this tradition, the more elegant and decorous manner of Virgil (together with the Roman poet's emphasis on divine destiny, piety and imperial responsibility) has offered a sounder model of the elevated dignity supposedly proper to the epic genre, than the explosive vehemence and down-to-earth particularity of Homer.

An alternative critical tradition has, however, relished the very aspects of Homer's art which others have responded to so warily. In antiquity, 'Longinus' and Dionysius of Halicarnassus praised Homer for the spellbinding and awe-inspiring sublimity of his dramatic conceptions, and for his use of the plainest diction and most commonplace details to uniquely moving effect. These criticisms were later echoed and reinforced by such commentators as Erasmus (in his expression of delight at Homer's use of everyday particulars to evoke 'the gentle emotions'), Boileau (in his praise of Homer's fiery vehemence and pathos), Goethe (in his endorsement of the Homeric vision of human life as hell-on-earth), Lessing (in his enthusiasm for the breadth of human sympathy displayed in Homer's characterization), Matthew Arnold (in his account of the 'rapidity', 'plainness' and 'nobility' of the Homeric style), and Simone Weil (in her sober celebration of Homer's clearsighted and impartial presentation of the miseries of war).

Of the English responses to Homer, none is more detailed and passionately committed than that of Alexander Pope, whose translations (*Iliad*, 1715–20; *Odyssey*, with the collaboration of William Broome and Elijah Fenton, 1725–6) are used in this selection. Commentators have often emphasized the ways in which the style and ethos of Pope's versions differs from that of their originals – contrasting, for example, the decorous rhetoric and diction of Pope's rhyming couplets with the looser syntax and plainer vocabulary of Homer's unrhymed hexameters, and noting those places where Pope seems intent on 'accommodating' Homer's alien psychology, morality and theology to models with which his readers were more familiar.

But, in voicing such criticisms, the critics tend to forget the overwhelming advantages which Pope's versions have over all others. Pope's *Iliad* is, first and foremost, the only English version of Homer which is an unequivocally great English poem in its own right. (The collaborative *Odyssey* is much less consistent, but nevertheless has many passages of high quality). The excellence of Pope's version resides, moreover, in far more than its rhetorical eloquence and the melodiousness of its versification. For Pope, reading Homer was a uniquely absorbing and transporting experience. 'No man of a true poetical spirit,' he wrote, 'is master of himself while he reads [Homer]. What he writes is of the most animated nature imaginable; everything moves, everything lives, and is put into action; . . . the reader is hurried out of himself by the force of the poet's imagination, and turns in one place to a hearer, in another to a spectator.' In his renderings, Pope lavished every resource of his critical intelligence and verbal artistry on the re-imagination, and vivid re-creation in a coherent and plausible English idiom, of the 'animated' 'force' of Homer's narratives, the compelling power of his speeches, and the 'daring' and 'glowing' 'energy' of his metaphors and similes. Pope's commitment to re-creating the 'fire' of Homer's narratives was simultaneously, and of necessity, a commitment to rendering plausible the network of values, relationships, psychological motives and theological beliefs which those narratives embody and imply. In *Local Knowledge* (1973), the anthropologist Clifford Geertz has written of the kind of translation which 'is not simple recasting of others' ways of putting things in terms of our own ways of putting them (that is the kind in which things get lost), but displaying the logic of their ways of putting them in the locutions of ours'. Geertz's formulation describes Pope's approach precisely, and allows one to see how the superficially un-Homeric elements in Pope's versions are not merely attempts to cut Homer down to eighteenth-century size, but parts of a complex and subtle process of inter-cultural negotiation, designed to mediate Homer's imaginative vision, in all its simultaneous familiarity and 'otherness', to readers of his own time and beyond. As the most vividly accomplished attempt to 'display the logic of' Homer's 'ways of putting things' to readers of English poetry, Pope's versions are the obvious first choice for a selection from Homer in the 'Everyman's Poetry' series.

Note on the Text and Selection

This selection attempts to collect as many of the most famous incidents, speeches and descriptions from the *Iliad* and *Odyssey* as can be viably accommodated in a volume of its size. Though it cannot provide the diverse and cumulative experience of reading two large epic narratives in their entirety, it attempts to be more than merely a collection of disconnected snippets: linking editorial narrations, designed to give the reader some sense of the part played by each extract within its larger context, allow the book to be read through consecutively as an introduction to (or reminder of) the complete poems, as well as to be dipped into more selectively.

Texts of Pope's translations are based on the last editions to be revised by the author: the 1743 edition of the *Iliad* and the 1725–6 edition of the *Odyssey*. Spelling and punctuation have been modernized. Line-numberings refer to the translations rather than their Greek originals. Of the parts of the *Odyssey* represented in this selection, initial reponsibility for Books 2, 6, 8, 11, 12, 16, and 23 was taken by Broome, and for Book 1 by Fenton. Both collaborators' work was, however, revised by Pope himself.

The Notes gloss (on their first appearance only) words, phrases and references that might puzzle a modern reader. The Glossary provides relevant information on persons (human and divine) and places in the narrative. Pope's translation generally uses Romanized forms: Greek equivalents, where appropriate, are supplied in brackets.

I am most grateful for the valuable help and encouragement which I have received, while working on this selection, from my colleagues, Charles Martindale and Tom Mason.

Homer

from **The Iliad**

from **Book 1**

Homer's subject: the wrath of Achilles.

> Achilles' wrath, to Greece the direful spring
> Of woes unnumbered, heavenly goddess, sing!
> That wrath which hurled to Pluto's gloomy reign
> The souls of mighty chiefs untimely slain;
> Whose limbs unburied on the naked shore   5
> Devouring dogs and hungry vultures tore.
> Since great Achilles and Atrides strove,
> Such was the sovereign doom, and such the will of Jove.

*In the tenth year of the Trojan War, the Greek army is afflicted by a
plague. Agamemnon is told that the pestilence will only be lifted if he
returns his captive maiden, Chryseis, to her father Chryses, the priest
of Apollo. Agamemnon agrees, but only on condition that he is paid
recompense, in the form of Achilles' captive maiden, Briseis. Achilles
protests vehemently.*

> At this, Pelides frowning stern, replied:
> 'O tyrant, armed with insolence and pride!
> Inglorious slave to interest, ever joined   195
> With fraud, unworthy of a royal mind.
> What generous Greek, obedient to thy word,
> Shall form an ambush, or shall lift the sword?
> What cause have I to war at thy decree?
> The distant Trojans never injured me.   200
> To Pthia's realms no hostile troops they led;
> Safe in her vales my warlike coursers fed;
> Far hence removed, the hoarse-resounding main
> And walls of rocks secure my native reign,
> Whose fruitful soil luxuriant harvests grace,   205

Rich in her fruits, and in her martial race.
Hither we sailed, a voluntary throng,
T' avenge a private, not a public wrong:
What else to Troy th' assembled nations draws,
But thine, ungrateful, and thy brother's cause?   210
Is this the pay our blood and toils deserve,
Disgraced and injured by the man we serve?
And dar'st thou threat to snatch my prize away,
Due to the deeds of many a dreadful day?
A prize as small, O tyrant, matched with thine,   215
As thy own actions if compared to mine!
Thine in each conquest is the wealthy prey,
Though mine the sweat and danger of the day.
Some trivial present to my ships I bear,
Or barren praises pay the wounds of war.   220
But know, proud monarch, I'm thy slave no more;
My fleet shall waft me to Thessalia's shore.
Left by Achilles on the Trojan plain,
What spoils, what conquests shall Atrides gain?'
        To this the king: 'Fly, mighty warrior, fly!   225
Thy aid we need not, and thy threats defy.
There want not chiefs in such a cause to fight,
And Jove himself shall guard a monarch's right.
Of all the kings (the gods' distinguished care)
To power superior none such hatred bear: 230
Strife and debate thy restless soul employ,
And wars and horrors are thy savage joy.
If thou hast strength, 'twas heaven that strength bestowed,
For know, vain man, thy valour is from God!
Haste, launch thy vessels, fly with speed away,   235
Rule thy own realms with arbitrary sway:
I heed thee not, but prize at equal rate
Thy short-lived friendship and thy groundless hate.
Go, threat thy earth-born Myrmidons; but here
'Tis mine to threaten, prince, and thine to fear.   240
Know, if the god the beauteous dame demand,
My bark shall waft her to her native land;
But then prepare, imperious prince, prepare,
Fierce as thou art, to yield thy captive fair:
Ev'n in thy tent I'll seize the blooming prize,   245

Thy loved Briseis with the radiant eyes.
Hence shalt thou prove my might, and curse the hour
Thou stood'st a rival of imperial power;
And hence to all our host it shall be known
That kings are subject to the gods alone!'   250
       Achilles heard, with grief and rage oppressed,
His heart swelled high, and laboured in his breast.
Distracting thoughts by turns his bosom ruled,
Now fired by wrath, and now by reason cooled:
That prompts his hand to draw the deadly sword,   255
Force through the Greeks, and pierce their haughty lord,
This whispers soft his vengeance to control,
And calm the rising tempest of his soul.
Just as in anguish of suspense he stayed,
While half-unsheathed appeared the glittering blade,   260
Minerva swift descended from above,
Sent by the sister and the wife of Jove
(For both the princes claimed her equal care);
Behind she stood, and by the golden hair
Achilles seized, to him alone confessed;   265
A sable cloud concealed her from the rest.
He sees, and sudden to the goddess cries,
Known by the flames that sparkle from her eyes.
       'Descends Minerva, in her guardian care,
A heavenly witness of the wrongs I bear   270
From Atreus' son? Then let those eyes that view
The daring crime behold the vengeance too!'
       'Forbear!' the progeny of Jove replies,
'To calm thy fury I forsake the skies:
Let great Achilles, to the gods resigned,   275
To reason yield the empire o'er his mind.
By awful Juno this command is given;
The king and you are both the care of heaven.
The force of keen reproaches let him feel,
But sheathe, obedient, thy revenging steel.   280
For I pronounce – and trust a heavenly power –
Thy injured honour has its fated hour,
When the proud monarch shall thy arms implore,
And bribe thy friendship with a boundless store.
Then let revenge no longer bear the sway,   285

Command thy passions, and the gods obey.'
          To her Pelides: 'With regardful ear
'Tis just, O goddess, I thy dictates hear.
Hard as it is, my vengeance I suppress:
Those who revere the gods, the gods will bless.'   290
          He said, observant of the blue-eyed maid;
Then in the sheath returned the shining blade.
The goddess swift to high Olympus flies,
And joins the sacred Senate of the skies.
          Nor yet the rage his boiling breast forsook,   295
Which thus redoubling on Atrides broke:
'O monster, mixed of insolence and fear,
Thou dog in forehead, but in heart a deer!
When wert thou known in ambushed fights to dare,
Or nobly face the horrid front of war?   300
'Tis ours, the chance of fighting fields to try,
Thine to look on, and bid the valiant die.
So much 'tis safer through the camp to go,
And rob a subject, than despoil a foe.
Scourge of thy people, violent and base!   305
Sent in Jove's anger on a slavish race,
Who, lost to sense of generous freedom past,
Are tamed to wrongs, or this had been thy last.
Now by this sacred sceptre hear me swear,
Which never more shall leaves or blossoms bear,   310
Which severed from the trunk – as I from thee –
On the bare mountains left its parent tree;
This sceptre, formed by tempered steel to prove
An ensign of the delegates of Jove,
From whom the power of laws and justice springs –   315
Tremendous oath, inviolate to kings! –
By this I swear, when bleeding Greece again
Shall call Achilles, she shall call in vain.
When flushed with slaughter Hector comes, to spread
The purpled shore with mountains of the dead,   320
Then shalt thou mourn th' affront thy madness gave,
Forced to deplore, when impotent to save:
Then rage in bitterness of soul, to know
This act has made the bravest Greek thy foe!'
          He spoke; and, furious, hurled against the ground   325

His sceptre starred with golden studs around.
Then sternly silent sat; with like disdain,
The raging king returned his frowns again.

*Briseis is taken from Achilles. He goes down to the sea-shore and
protests vehemently to his mother, the sea-nymph Thetis, begging her
to petition the gods to humble the Greeks, in recompense for the injury
done to him. Jove agrees to her request, but their tête-à-tête is
witnessed by Juno, who jealously cross-questions her husband on his
return to Olympus.*

'Say, artful manager of heaven,' she cries,
'Who now partakes the secrets of the skies?
Thy Juno knows not the decrees of fate,   700
In vain the partner of imperial state.
What favourite goddess then those cares divides,
Which Jove in prudence from his consort hides?'
        To this the Thunderer: 'Seek not thou to find
The sacred counsels of almighty mind.   705
Involved in darkness lies the great decree,
Nor can the depths of fate be pierced by thee.
What fits thy knowledge, thou the first shalt know,
The first of gods above, and men below;
But thou, nor they, shall search the thoughts that roll   710
Deep in the close recesses of my soul.'
        Full on the sire the goddess of the skies
Rolled the large orbs of her majestic eyes,
And thus returned: 'Austere Saturnius, say,
From whence this wrath, or who controls thy sway?   715
Thy boundless will, for me, remains in force,
And all thy counsels take the destined course.
But 'tis for Greece I fear, for late was seen
In close consult, the silver-footed queen.
Jove to his Thetis nothing could deny,   720
Nor was the signal vain that shook the sky.
What fatal favour has the goddess won,
To grace her fierce, inexorable son?
Perhaps in Grecian blood to drench the plain,
And glut his vengeance with my people slain.'   725
        Then thus the god: 'Oh restless fate of pride,

That strives to learn what heaven resolves to hide;
Vain is the search, presumptuous and abhorred,
Anxious to thee, and odious to thy lord.
Let this suffice; th' immutable decree   730
No force can shake: what is, that ought to be.
Goddess submit, nor dare our will withstand,
But dread the power of this avenging hand;
Th'united strength of all the gods above
In vain resists th' omnipotence of Jove.'   735
          The Thunderer spoke, nor durst the queen reply;
A reverend horror silenced all the sky.
The feast disturbed with sorrow Vulcan saw;
His mother menaced, and the gods in awe;
Peace at his heart, and pleasure his design,   740
Thus interposed the architect divine:
          'The wretched quarrels of the mortal state
Are far unworthy, gods, of your debate!
Let men their days in senseless strife employ,
We in eternal peace and constant joy.   745
Thou, goddess-mother, with our sire comply,
Nor break the sacred union of the sky;
Lest, roused to rage, he shake the blessed abodes,
Launch the red lightning, and dethrone the gods.
If you submit, the Thunderer stands appeased;   750
The gracious power is willing to be pleased.'
          Thus Vulcan spoke; and rising with a bound,
The double bowl with sparkling nectar crowned,
Which held to Juno in a cheerful way,
'Goddess,' he cried, 'be patient and obey!   755
Dear as you are, if Jove his arm extend,
I can but grieve, unable to defend.
What god so daring in your aid to move,
Or lift his hand against the force of Jove?
Once in your cause I felt his matchless might,   760
Hurled headlong downward from th' ethereal height;
Tossed all the day in rapid circles round,
Nor till the sun descended, touched the ground.
Breathless I fell, in giddy motion lost;
The Sinthians raised me on the Lemnian coast.'   765
          He said, and to her hands the goblet heaved,

Which, with a smile, the white-armed queen received.
Then to the rest he filled; and, in his turn,
Each to his lips applied the nectared urn.
Vulcan with awkward grace his office plies,   770
And unextinguished laughter shakes the skies.
      Thus the blessed gods the genial day prolong,
In feasts ambrosial, and celestial song.
Apollo tuned the lyre; the Muses round
With voice alternate aid the silver sound.   775
Meantime the radiant sun, to mortal sight
Descending swift, rolled down the rapid light;
Then to their starry domes the gods depart,
The shining monuments of Vulcan's art:
Jove on his couch reclined his awful head,   780
And Juno slumbered on the golden bed.

from **Book 2**

Roused by a dream from Jove, Agamemnon resolves to lead the Greek army into battle without Achilles. Ulysses rallies the Greek forces. The one dissentient voice is that of Thersites.

      Thersites only clamoured in the throng,   255
Loquacious, loud, and turbulent of tongue;
Awed by no shame, by no respect controlled,
In scandal busy, in reproaches bold,
With witty malice studious to defame,
Scorn all his joy, and laughter all his aim;   260
But chief he gloried with licentious style
To lash the great, and monarchs to revile.
His figure such as might his soul proclaim;
One eye was blinking, and one leg was lame:
His mountain-shoulders half his breast o'erspread,   265
Thin hairs bestrewed his long misshapen head.
Spleen to mankind his envious heart possessed,
And much he hated all, but most the best;

Ulysses or Achilles still his theme;
But royal scandal his delight supreme.   270
Long had he lived the scorn of every Greek –
Vexed when he spoke, yet still they heard him speak.
Sharp was his voice, which in the shrillest tone,
Thus with injurious taunts attacked the throne:
      'Amidst the glories of so bright a reign,   275
What moves the great Atrides to complain?
'Tis thine whate'er the warrior's breast inflames,
The golden spoil, and thine the lovely dames.
With all the wealth our wars and blood bestow,
Thy tents are crowded, and thy chests o'erflow.   280
Thus at full ease, in heaps of riches rolled,
What grieves the monarch? Is it thirst of gold?
Say, shall we march with our unconquered powers,
(The Greeks and I) to Ilion's hostile towers,
And bring the race of royal bastards here,   285
For Troy to ransom at a price too dear?
But safer plunder thy own host supplies;
Say, would'st thou seize some valiant leader's prize?
Or, if thy heart to generous love be led,
Some captive fair, to bless thy kingly bed?   290
Whate'er our master craves, submit we must,
Plagued with his pride, or punished for his lust.
O women of Achaia, men no more,
Hence let us fly, and let him waste his store
In loves and pleasures on the Phrygian shore!   295
We may be wanted on some busy day,
When Hector comes, so great Achilles may.
From him he forced the prize we jointly gave,
From him, the fierce, the fearless, and the brave:
And durst he, as he ought, resent that wrong,   300
This mighty tyrant were no tyrant long.'
      Fierce from his seat, at this Ulysses springs,
In generous vengeance of the king of kings.
With indignation sparkling in his eyes
He views the wretch, and sternly thus replies: 305
'Peace, factious monster, born to vex the state,
With wrangling talents formed for foul debate:
Curb that impetuous tongue, nor rashly vain

And singly mad, asperse the sovereign reign.
Have we not known thee, slave, of all our host   310
The man who acts the least, upbraids the most?
Think not the Greeks to shameful flight to bring,
Nor let those lips profane the name of king.
For our return we trust the heavenly powers;
Be that their care; to fight like men be ours.   315
But grant the host with wealth the general load,
Except detraction, what hast thou bestowed?
Suppose some hero should his spoils resign,
Art thou that hero, could those spoils be thine?
Gods! let me perish on this hateful shore,   320
And let these eyes behold my son no more,
If, on thy next offence, this hand forbear
To strip those arms thou ill deserv'st to wear,
Expel the council where our princes meet,
And send thee scourged, and howling through the fleet!'   325
         He said, and, cowering as the dastard bends,
The weighty sceptre on his back descends:
On the round bunch the bloody tumours rise;
The tears spring starting from his haggard eyes.
Trembling he sat, and, shrunk in abject fears,   330
From his vile visage wiped the scalding tears.

The Greek troops assemble.

         As on some mountain, through the lofty grove,
The crackling flames ascend and blaze above;   535
The fires expanding as the winds arise,
Shoot their long beams, and kindle half the skies:
So from the polished arms, and brazen shields,
A gleamy splendour flashed along the fields.
Not less their number than th' embodied cranes,   540
Or milk-white swans in Asius' watery plains,
That o'er the windings of Caÿster's springs
Stretch their long necks, and clap their rustling wings,
Now tower aloft, and course in airy rounds,
Now light with noise – with noise the field resounds.   545
Thus numerous and confused, extending wide,
The legions crowd Scamander's flowery side,

With rushing troops the plains are covered o'er,
And thundering footsteps shake the sounding shore.
Along the river's level meads they stand,   550
Thick as in spring the flowers adorn the land,
Or leaves the trees; or thick as insects play,
The wandering nation of a summer's day,
That, drawn by milky steams, at evening hours,
In gathered swarms surround the rural bowers;   555
From pail to pail with busy murmur run
The gilded legions, glittering in the sun:
So thronged, so close, the Grecian squadrons stood
In radiant arms, and thirst for Trojan blood.
Each leader now his scattered force conjoins   560
In close array, and forms the deepening lines.
Not with more ease, the skilful shepherd-swain
Collects his flock from thousands on the plain.
The king of kings, majestically tall,
Towers o'er his armies, and outshines them all: 565
Like some proud bull that round the pastures leads
His subject-herds, the monarch of the meads.
Great as the gods th' exalted chief was seen,
His strength like Neptune, and like Mars his mien;
Jove o'er his eyes celestial glories spread,   570
And dawning conquest played around his head.

from **Book 3**

*Paris agrees to engage in single combat with Menelaus to determine
the outcome of the war. Iris summons Helen to view the fight from the
battlements of Troy.*

            Meantime, to beauteous Helen from the skies   165
The various goddess of the rainbow flies,
Like fair Laodicè in form and face,
The loveliest nymph of Priam's royal race.
Her in the palace, at her loom she found;

The golden web her own sad story crowned,   170
The Trojan wars she weaved, herself the prize,
And the dire triumphs of her fatal eyes.
To whom the goddess of the painted bow:
'Approach, and view the wondrous scene below!
Each hardy Greek and valiant Trojan knight,   175
So dreadful late, and furious for the fight,
Now rest their spears, or lean upon their shields;
Ceased is the war, and silent all the fields.
Paris alone and Sparta's king advance,
In single fight to toss the beamy lance;   180
Each met in arms, the fate of combat tries,
Thy love the motive, and thy charms the prize.'
            This said, the many-coloured maid inspires
Her husband's love, and wakes her former fires;
Her country, parents, all that once were dear,   185
Rush to her thought, and force a tender tear.
O'er her fair face a snowy veil she threw,
And, softly sighing, from the loom withdrew.
Her handmaids Clymenè and Aethra wait
Her silent footsteps to the Scaean gate.   190
            There sat the seniors of the Trojan race,
Old Priam's chiefs, and most in Priam's grace;
The king the first, Thymaetes at his side,
Lampus and Clytius, long in council tried,
Panthus, and Hicetäon, once the strong,   195
And next the wisest of the reverend throng,
Antenor grave, and sage Ucalegon,
Leaned on the walls, and basked before the sun;
Chiefs, who no more in bloody fights engage,
But wise through time, and narrative with age,   200
In summer days like grasshoppers rejoice,
A bloodless race, that send a feeble voice.
These, when the Spartan queen approached the tower,
In secret owned resistless beauty's power:
They cried, 'No wonder such celestial charms   205
For nine long years have set the world in arms;
What winning graces! What majestic mien!
She moves a goddess, and she looks a queen!
Yet hence, O heaven, convey that fatal face,

And from destruction save the Trojan race!'   210
      The good old Priam welcomed her, and cried,
'Approach my child, and grace thy father's side:
See on the plain thy Grecian spouse appears,
The friends and kindred of thy former years.
No crime of thine our present sufferings draws,   215
Not thou, but heaven's disposing will, the cause;
The gods these armies and this force employ,
The hostile gods conspire the fate of Troy!'

Helen shows Priam the principal Greek warriors from the battlements.
She cannot, however, see her brothers, Castor and Pollux:

'The rest I know, and could in order name,
All valiant chiefs, and men of mighty fame.   300
Yet two are wanting of the numerous train,
Whom long my eyes have sought, but sought in vain;
Castor and Pollux, first in martial force,
One bold on foot, and one renowned for horse;
My brothers these; the same our native shore,   305
One house contained us, as one mother bore.
Perhaps the chiefs, from warlike toils at ease,
For distant Troy refused to sail the seas:
Perhaps their sword some nobler quarrel draws,
Ashamed to combat in their sister's cause.'   310
      So spoke the fair, nor knew her brothers' doom,
Wrapped in the cold embraces of the tomb;
Adorned with honours in their native shore,
Silent they slept, and heard of wars no more.

Paris fights Menelaus, and is about to be killed, when Venus spirits
him from the battlefield in a veil of cloud. Venus, disguised, summons
Helen to Paris' bedchamber.

      She spoke, and Helen's secret soul was moved;
She scorned the champion, but the man she loved.
Fair Venus' neck, her eyes that sparkled fire,
And breast revealed the queen of soft desire.   490
Struck with her presence, straight the lively red
Forsook her cheek; and, trembling, thus she said:

'Then is it still thy pleasure to deceive?
And woman's frailty always to believe?
Say, to new nations must I cross the main,   495
Or carry wars to some soft Asian plain?
For whom must Helen break her second vow?
What other Paris is thy darling now?
Left to Atrides, victor in the strife,
An odious conquest and a captive wife,   500
Hence let me sail: and if thy Paris bear
My absence ill, let Venus ease his care.
A handmaid goddess at his side to wait,
Renounce the glories of thy heavenly state,
Be fixed for ever to the Trojan shore,   505
His spouse, or slave, and mount the skies no more.
For me, to lawless love no longer led,
I scorn the coward, and detest his bed;
Else should I merit everlasting shame,
And keen reproach, from every Phrygian dame: 510
Ill suits it now the joys of love to know,
Too deep my anguish, and too wild my woe.'
        Then thus, incensed, the Paphian queen replies:
'Obey the power from whom thy glories rise:
Should Venus leave thee, every charm must fly,   515
Fade from thy cheek, and languish in thy eye.
Cease to provoke me, lest I make thee more
The world's aversion than their love before.
Now the bright prize for which mankind engage,
Then the sad victim of the public rage.'   520
        At this, the fairest of her sex obeyed,
And veiled her blushes in a silken shade;
Unseen, and silent, from the train she moves,
Led by the goddess of the smiles and loves.
Arrived, and entered at the palace gate,   525
The maids officious round their mistress wait,
Then, all dispersing, various tasks attend;
The queen and goddess to the prince ascend.
Full in her Paris' sight the Queen of Love
Had placed the beauteous progeny of Jove;   530
Where, as he viewed her charms, she turned away
Her glowing eyes, and thus began to say:

'Is this the chief, who lost to sense of shame
Late fled the field, and yet survives his fame?
Oh hadst thou died beneath the righteous sword   535
Of that brave man whom once I called my lord!
The boaster Paris oft desired the day
With Sparta's king to meet in single fray:
Go now, once more thy rival's rage excite,
Provoke Atrides and renew the fight –   540
Yet Helen bids thee stay, lest thou unskilled
Should'st fall an easy conquest on the field.'
    The prince replies: 'Ah cease, divinely fair,
Nor add reproaches to the wounds I bear;
This day the foe prevailed by Pallas' power;   545
We yet may vanquish in a happier hour.
There want not gods to favour us above;
But let the business of our life be love.
These softer moments let delights employ,
And kind embraces snatch the hasty joy.   550
Not thus I loved thee, when from Sparta's shore
My forced, my willing heavenly prize I bore,
When first entranced in Cranaë's isle I lay,
Mixed with thy soul, and all dissolved away.'
    Thus having spoke, th' enamoured Phrygian boy   555
Rushed to the bed, impatient for the joy.
Him Helen followed slow with bashful charms,
And clasped the blooming hero in her arms.

from **Book 4**

The truce between the Greeks and Trojans is breached, through the agency of Jove. As the battle recommences, Agamemnon displays valour and leadership, and rouses the Greek warriors to combat. Thick fighting ensues.

As when the winds, ascending by degrees,
First move the whitening surface of the seas,
The billows float in order to the shore,   480
The wave behind rolls on the wave before;
Till, with the growing storm, the deeps arise,
Foam o'er the rocks, and thunder to the skies:
So to the fight the thick battalions throng,
Shields urged on shields, and men drove men along.   485
Sedate and silent move the numerous bands;
No sound, no whisper, but the chief's commands,
Those only heard; with awe the rest obey,
As if some god had snatched their voice away.
Not so the Trojans, from their host ascends   490
A general shout that all the region rends.
As when the fleecy flocks unnumbered stand
In wealthy folds, and wait the milker's hand,
The hollow vales incessant bleating fills,
The lambs reply from all the neighbouring hills: 495
Such clamours rose from various nations round,
Mixed was the murmur, and confused the sound.
Each host now joins, and each a god inspires,
These Mars incites, and those Minerva fires.
Pale Flight around, and dreadful Terror reign;   500
And Discord raging bathes the purple plain;
Discord, dire sister of the slaughtering power,
Small at her birth, but rising every hour,
While scarce the skies her horrid head can bound,
She stalks on earth, and shakes the world around;   505
The nations bleed where'er her steps she turns,
The groan still deepens, and the combat burns.
Now shield with shield, with helmet helmet closed,
To armour armour, lance to lance opposed,

Host against host with shadowy squadrons drew,   510
The sounding darts in iron tempests flew,
Victors and vanquished joined promiscuous cries,
And shrilling shouts and dying groans arise;
With streaming blood the slippery fields are dyed,
And slaughtered heroes swell the dreadful tide.   515
        As torrents roll, increased by numerous rills,
With rage impetuous down their echoing ills,
Rush to the vales, and poured along the plain,
Roar through a thousand channels to the main;
The distant shepherd trembling hears the sound: 520
So mix both hosts, and so their cries rebound.

from **Book 5**

Diomedes kills many Trojans, and even wounds the goddess Venus.
Hector rallies the Trojans, who stand to face the Greek army, which is
seen approaching from a distance.

        As when on Ceres' sacred floor the swain
Spreads the wide fan to clear the golden grain,
And the light chaff, before the breezes borne,
Ascends in clouds from off the heapy corn;
The grey dust, rising with collected winds,   615
Drives o'er the barn, and whitens all the hinds.
So white with dust the Grecian host appears,
From trampling steeds, and thundering charioteers.
The dusky clouds from laboured earth arise,
And roll in smoking volumes to the skies.   620
Mars hovers o'er them with his sable shield,
And adds new horrors to the darkened field.

Battle is joined:

        Embodied close, the labouring Grecian train
The fiercest shock of charging hosts sustain;

Unmoved and silent, the whole war they wait,
Serenely dreadful, and as fixed as fate.   640
So when th' embattled clouds in dark array
Along the skies their gloomy lines display,
When now the North his boisterous rage has spent,
And peaceful sleeps the liquid element,
The low-hung vapours, motionless and still,   645
Rest on the summits of the shaded hill,
Till the mass scatters as the winds arise,
Dispersed and broken through the ruffled skies.

from **Book 6**

After more fighting, Hector returns to Troy, and exhorts Hecuba to
pray to Minerva to avert Diomedes' continuing attack. She does so, but
the Trojans' prayers are rejected. Meanwhile, Hector goes in search of
his wife, Andromache, and bids her farewell before returning to the
battle.

Hector, this heard, returned without delay;
Swift through the town he trod his former way,
Through streets of palaces and walks of state,   490
And met the mourner at the Scaean gate.
With haste to meet him sprung the joyful fair,
His blameless wife, Aëtion's wealthy heir
(Cilician Thebè great Aëtion swayed,
And Hippoplacus' wide-extended shade);   495
The nurse stood near, in whose embraces pressed
His only hope hung smiling at her breast,
Whom each soft charm and early grace adorn,
Fair as the new-born star that gilds the morn.
To this loved infant Hector gave the name   500
Scamandrius, from Scamander's honoured stream;
Astyanax the Trojans called the boy,
From his great father, the defence of Troy.
Silent the warrior smiled, and, pleased, resigned

To tender passions all his mighty mind;　　　　　505
His beauteous princess cast a mournful look,
Hung on his hand, and then dejected spoke;
Her bosom laboured with a boding sigh,
And the big tear stood trembling in her eye:
　　　'Too daring prince! Ah, whither dost thou run?　510
Ah too forgetful of thy wife and son!
And think'st thou not how wretched we shall be,
A widow I, an helpless orphan he!
For sure such courage length of life denies,
And thou must fall, thy virtue's sacrifice.　　　　515
Greece in her single heroes strove in vain;
Now hosts oppose thee, and thou must be slain!
Oh grant me, gods, ere Hector meets his doom,
All I can ask of heaven, an early tomb!
So shall my days in one sad tenor run,　　　　　520
And end with sorrows as they first begun.
No parent now remains my griefs to share,
No father's aid, no mother's tender care.
The fierce Achilles wrapped our walls in fire,
Layed Thebè waste, and slew my warlike sire!　　525
His fate compassion in the victor bred;
Stern as he was, he yet revered the dead,
His radiant arms preserved from hostile spoil,
And laid him decent on the funeral pile;
Then raised a mountain where his bones were burned,　530
The mountain nymphs the rural tomb adorned,
Jove's sylvan daughters bade their elms bestow
A barren shade, and in his honour grow.
　　　By the same arm my seven brave brothers fell,
In one sad day beheld the gates of hell,　　　　535
While the fat herds and snowy flocks they fed,
Amid their fields the hapless heroes bled!
My mother lived to bear the victor's bands,
The queen of Hippoplacia's sylvan lands;
Redeemed too late, she scarce beheld again　　　540
Her pleasing empire and her native plain,
When, ah, oppressed by life-consuming woe,
She fell a victim to Diana's bow.
　　　Yet while my Hector still survives, I see

My father, mother, brethren, all, in thee.   545
Alas! my parents, brothers, kindred, all
Once more will perish if my Hector fall.
Thy wife, thy infant, in thy danger share:
Oh prove a husband's and a father's care!
That quarter most the skilful Greeks annoy,   550
Where yon wild fig trees join the wall of Troy:
Thou, from this tower defend th' important post;
There Agamemnon points his dreadful host,
That pass Tydides, Ajax strive to gain,
And there the vengeful Spartan fires his train.   555
Thrice our bold foes the fierce attack have given,
Or led by hopes, or dictated from heaven.
Let others in the field their arms employ,
But stay my Hector here, and guard his Troy.'
          The chief replied, 'That post shall be my care,   560
Not that alone, but all the works of war.
How would the sons of Troy, in arms renowned,
And Troy's proud dames whose garments sweep the ground
Attaint the lustre of my former name,
Should Hector basely quit the field of fame?   565
My early youth was bred to martial pains,
My soul impels me to th'embattled plains;
Let me be foremost to defend the throne,
And guard my father's glories, and my own.
          Yet come it will, the day decreed by fates –   570
How my heart trembles while my tongue relates! –
The day when thou, imperial Troy, must bend,
And see thy warriors fall, thy glories end!
And yet no dire presage so wounds my mind,
My mother's death, the ruin of my kind,   575
Not Priam's hoary hairs defiled with gore,
Not all my brothers gasping on the shore,
As thine, Andromache, thy griefs I dread;
I see thee trembling, weeping, captive led!
In Argive looms our battles to design,   580
And woes, of which so large a part was thine!
To bear the victor's hard commands, or bring
The weight of waters from Hyperia's spring.
There, while you groan beneath the load of life,

They cry, "Behold the mighty Hector's wife!"   585
Some haughty Greek, who lives thy tears to see,
Embitters all thy woes by naming me.
The thoughts of glory past, and present shame,
A thousand griefs shall waken at the name!
May I lie cold before that dreadful day,   590
Pressed with a load of monumental clay!
Thy Hector, wrapped in everlasting sleep,
Shall neither hear thee sigh, nor see thee weep.'
          Thus having spoke, th' illustrious chief of Troy
Stretched his fond arms to clasp the lovely boy.   595
The babe clung crying to his nurse's breast,
Scared at the dazzling helm and nodding crest.
With secret pleasure each fond parent smiled,
And Hector hasted to relieve his child,
The glittering terrors from his brows unbound,   600
And placed the beaming helmet on the ground;
Then kissed the child, and lifting high in air,
Thus to the gods preferred a father's prayer:
          'O thou whose glory fills th' ethereal throne,
And all ye deathless powers, protect my son!   605
Grant him, like me, to purchase just renown,
To guard the Trojans, to defend the crown,
Against his country's foes the war to wage,
And rise, the Hector of the future age!
So when, triumphant from successful toils   610
Of heroes slain he bears the reeking spoils,
Whole hosts may hail him with deserved acclaim,
And say, "This chief transcends his father's fame",
While pleased amidst the general shouts of Troy,
His mother's conscious heart o'erflows with joy.'   615
          He spoke, and, fondly gazing on her charms,
Restored the pleasing burden to her arms;
Soft on her fragrant breast the babe she laid,
Hushed to repose, and with a smile surveyed.
The troubled pleasure soon chastised by fear,   620
She mingled with the smile a tender tear.
The softened chief with kind compassion viewed,
And dried the falling drops, and thus pursued:
          'Andromache, my soul's far better part,

Why with untimely sorrows heaves thy heart?   625
No hostile hand can antedate my doom,
Till fate condemns me to the silent tomb.
Fixed is the term to all the race of earth,
And such the hard condition of our birth.
No force can then resist, no flight can save,   630
All sink alike, the fearful and the brave.
No more – but hasten to thy tasks at home,
There guide the spindle, and direct the loom;
Me glory summons to the martial scene,
The field of combat is the sphere for men.   635
Where heroes war, the foremost place I claim,
The first in danger as the first in fame.'
        Thus having said, the glorious chief resumes
His towery helmet, black with shading plumes.
His princess parts with a prophetic sigh,   640
Unwilling parts, and oft reverts her eye
That streamed at every look: then, moving slow,
Sought her own palace, and indulged her woe.
There, while her tears deplored the godlike man,
Through all her train the soft infection ran;   645
The pious maids their mingled sorrows shed,
And mourn the living Hector, as the dead.

After a single combat between Ajax and Hector, which is interrupted
by nightfall, a second truce is arranged, for the cremation of the dead.
The Greeks build fortifications to protect their camp and ships.

from **Book 8**

The next day, battle recommences, with much carnage on both sides. That night, Hector orders watch-fires to be built, to ensure that the Greeks do not escape unnoticed, or attack Troy while it is undefended.

The troops exulting sat in order round,   685
And beaming fires illumined all the ground;
As when the moon, refulgent lamp of night,
O'er heavens clear azure spreads her sacred light,
When not a breath disturbs the deep serene,
And not a cloud o'ercasts the solemn scene;   690
Around her throne the vivid planets roll,
And stars unnumbered gild the glowing pole,
O'er the dark trees a yellower verdure shed,
And tip with silver every mountain's head;
Then shine the vales, the rocks in prospect rise,   695
A flood of glory bursts from all the skies.
The conscious swains, rejoicing in the sight,
Eye the blue vault, and bless the useful light:
So many flames before proud Ilion blaze,
And lighten glimmering Xanthus with their rays.   700
The long reflections of the distant fires
Gleam on the walls, and tremble on the spires.
A thousand piles the dusky horrors gild,
And shoot a shady lustre o'er the field.
Full fifty guards each flaming pile attend,   705
Whose umbered arms, by fits, thick flashes send.
Loud neigh the coursers o'er their heaps of corn,
And ardent warriors wait the rising morn.

from **Book 9**

Prompted by Nestor, Agamemnon admits that he has wronged Achilles, and undertakes to make reparation. An embassy is sent to Achilles' tent, and is received hospitably. Ulysses begs Achilles to return to the fight: Agamemnon has offered to return Briseis, untouched, along with other gifts. But Achilles defiantly rejects Agamemnon's offer:

      'Then thus in short my fixed resolves attend,
    Which nor Atrides, nor his Greeks can bend;   415
    Long toils, long perils in their cause I bore,
    But now th' unfruitful glories charm no more.
    Fight or not fight, a like reward we claim,
    The wretch and hero find their prize the same;
    Alike regretted in the dust he lies   420
    Who yields ignobly, or who bravely dies.
    Of all my dangers, all my glorious pains,
    A life of labours, lo, what fruit remains!
    As the bold bird her helpless young attends,
    From danger guards them, and from want defends;   425
    In search of prey she wings the spacious air,
    And with th' untasted food supplies her care:
    For thankless Greece such hardships have I braved,
    Her wives, her infants by my labours saved;
    Long sleepless nights in heavy arms I stood,   430
    And sweat laborious days in dust and blood.
    I sacked twelve ample cities on the main,
    And twelve lay smoking on the Trojan plain;
    Then at Atrides' haughty feet were laid
    The wealth I gathered, and the spoils I made.   435
    Your mighty monarch these in peace possessed;
    Some few my soldiers had, himself the rest.
    Some present, too, to every prince was paid,
    And every prince enjoys the gift he made;
    I only must refund, of all his train: 440
    See what pre-eminence our merits gain!
    My spoil alone his greedy soul delights;
    My spouse alone must bless his lustful nights.

The woman, let him, as he may, enjoy;
But what's the quarrel then of Greece to Troy?   445
What to these shores th' assembled nations draws,
What calls for vengeance, but a woman's cause?
Are fair endowments and a beauteous face
Beloved by none but those of Atreus' race?
The wife whom choice and passion both approve   450
Sure every wise and worthy man will love.
Nor did my fair one less distinction claim;
Slave as she was, my soul adored the dame.
Wronged in my love, all proffers I disdain;
Deceived for once, I trust not kings again.   455
Ye have my answer – what remains to do,
Your king, Ulysses, may consult with you.
What needs he the defence this arm can make?
Has he not walls no human force can shake?
Has he not fenced his guarded navy round   460
With piles, with ramparts, and a trench profound?
And will not these (the wonders he has done)
Repel the rage of Priam's single son?
There was a time – 'twas when for Greece I fought –
When Hector's prowess no such wonders wrought;   465
He kept the verge of Troy, nor dared to wait
Achilles' fury at the Scaean gate;
He tried it once, and scarce was saved by fate.
But now those ancient enmities are o'er;
Tomorrow we the favouring gods implore;   470
Then shall you see our parting vessels crowned,
And hear with oars the Hellespont resound.
The third day hence, shall Pthia greet our sails,
If mighty Neptune send propitious gales;
Pthia to her Achilles shall restore   475
The wealth he left for this detested shore.
Thither the spoils of this long war shall pass,
The ruddy gold, the steel, and shining brass;
My beauteous captives thither I'll convey,
And all that rests of my unravished prey.   480
One only valued gift your tyrant gave,
And that resumed: the fair Lyrnessian slave.
Then tell him, loud, that all the Greeks may hear;

And learn to scorn the wretch they basely fear –
For, armed in impudence, mankind he braves,   485
And meditates new cheats on all his slaves:
Though shameless as he is, to face these eyes
Is what he dares not; if he dares, he dies –
Tell him, all terms, all commerce I decline,
Nor share his council, nor his battle join;   490
For once deceived, was his; but twice, were mine . . .
Life is not to be bought with heaps of gold;
Not all Apollo's Pythian treasures hold,   525
Or Troy once held, in peace and pride of sway,
Can bribe the poor possession of a day!
Lost herds and treasures we by arms regain,
And steeds unrivalled on the dusty plain;
But from our lips the vital spirit fled   530
Returns no more to wake the silent dead.
My fates long since by Thetis were disclosed,
And each alternate, life or fame proposed:
Here, if I stay, before the Trojan town,
Short is my date, but deathless my renown;   535
If I return, I quit immortal praise
For years on years, and long-extended days.
Convinced, though late, I find my fond mistake,
And warn the Greeks the wiser choice to make:
To quit these shores, their native seats enjoy,   540
Nor hope the fall of heaven-defended Troy.
Jove's arm, displayed, asserts her from the skies;
Her hearts are strengthened, and her glories rise.
Go then, to Greece report our fixed design;
Bid all your councils, all your armies join,   545
Let all your forces, all your arts conspire,
To save the ships, the troops, the chiefs, from fire.
One stratagem has failed, and others will:
Ye find, Achilles is unconquered still.'

*Phoenix, Achilles' former tutor, attempts to persuade Achilles to relent
by heeding prayers.*

       'The gods (the only great, and only wise)   620
Are moved by offerings, vows, and sacrifice;
Offending man their high compassion wins,
And daily prayers attone for daily sins.
Prayers are Jove's daughters, of celestial race,
Lame are their feet, and wrinkled is their face;   625
With humble mien, and with dejected eyes,
Constant they follow where injustice flies:
Injustice swift, erect, and unconfined
Sweeps the wide earth, and tramples o'er mankind,
While Prayers, to heal her wrongs, move slow behind.   630
Who hears these daughters of almighty Jove,
For him they mediate to the throne above;
When man rejects the humble suit they make,
The sire revenges for the daughters' sake,
From Jove commissioned, fierce Injustice then   635
Descends, to punish unrelenting men.
Oh let not headlong passion bear the sway;
These reconciling goddesses obey!
Due honours to the seed of Jove belong;
Due honours calm the fierce, and bend the strong.   640
Were these not paid thee by the terms we bring,
Were rage still harboured in the haughty king,
Nor Greece nor all her fortunes should engage
Thy friend to plead against so just a rage.
But since what honour asks, the general sends,   645
And sends by those whom most thy heart commends,
The best and noblest of the Grecian train,
Permit not these to sue, and sue in vain!'

*Achilles, however, remains adamant. The Greeks agree to resume the
fight without him. Agamemnon and Ajax perform mighty deeds of
valour.*

from **Book 12**

Hector leads an attack on the Greeks, who retire behind their ramparts. The greater and lesser Ajaxes rally the Greeks and volleys of stones are discharged by both sides.

        Their ardour kindles all the Grecian powers,
And now the stones descend in heavier showers: 330
As when high Jove his sharp artillery forms,
And opes his cloudy magazine of storms;
In winter's bleak, uncomfortable reign,
A snowy inundation hides the plain;
He stills the winds, and bids the skies to sleep;   335
Then pours the silent tempest, thick and deep;
And first the mountain tops are covered o'er,
Then the green fields, and then the sandy shore;
Bent with the weight the nodding woods are seen,
And one bright waste hides all the works of men.   340
The circling seas alone absorbing all
Drink the dissolving fleeces as they fall:
So from each side increased the stony rain,
And the white ruin rises o'er the plain.

Jove's son, the Lycian warrior Sarpedon, exhorts his friend Glaucus to join him in attempting to breach the Greek fortifications:

        'Why boast we, Glaucus, our extended reign,
Where Xanthus' streams enrich the Lycian plain,
Our numerous herds that range the fruitful field,
And hills where vines their purple harvest yield,
Our foaming bowls with purer nectar crowned,   375
Our feasts enhanced with music's sprightly sound?
Why on those shores are we with joy surveyed,
Admired as heroes, and as gods obeyed,
Unless great acts superior merit prove,
And vindicate the bounteous powers above?   380
'Tis ours, the dignity they give to grace,
The first in valour, as the first in place;
That when with wondering eyes our martial bands

Behold our deeds transcending our commands,
Such, they may cry, deserve the sovereign state,   385
Whom those that envy dare not imitate!
Could all our care elude the gloomy grave,
Which claims no less the fearful than the brave,
For lust of fame I should not vainly dare
In fighting fields, nor urge thy soul to war.   390
But since, alas, ignoble age must come,
Disease, and death's inexorable doom,
The life which others pay, let us bestow,
And give to fame what we to nature owe.
Brave though we fall, and honoured if we live,   395
Or let us glory gain, or glory give!'

from **Book 13**

*Neptune inspires the Greeks to resist the Trojan attack. The fighting
continues, between the Greek wall and the sea shore. Hector performs
great feats of valour.*

Thus breathing death, in terrible array,
The close-compacted legions urged their way.
Fierce they drove on, impatient to destroy;
Troy charged the first, and Hector first of Troy.   190
As from some mountain's craggy forehead torn
A rock's round fragment flies, with fury borne,
Which from the stubborn stone a torrent rends,
Precipitate the ponderous mass descends;
From steep to steep the rolling ruin bounds,   195
At every shock the crackling wood resounds;
Still gathering force, it smokes, and, urged amain,
Whirls, leaps, and thunders down, impetuous to the plain,
There stops: so Hector; their whole force he proved,
Resistless when he raged, and when he stopped, unmoved.   200

from **Book 14**

Juno meditates on how she might best prevent Jove from stopping Neptune's support of the Greeks. She decides on seduction.

      Swift to her bright apartment she repairs,
Sacred to dress, and beauty's pleasing cares:
With skill divine had Vulcan formed the bower,
Safe from access of each intruding power.
Touched with her secret key, the doors unfold;   195
Self-closed, behind her shut the valves of gold.
Here first she bathes; and round her body pours
Soft oils of fragrance, and ambrosial showers.
The winds, perfumed, the balmy gale convey
Through heaven, through earth, and all th' aërial way; 200
Spirit divine, whose exhalation greets
The sense of gods with more than mortal sweets!
Thus while she breathed of heaven, with decent pride
Her artful hands the radiant tresses tied;
Part on her head in shining ringlets rolled,   205
Part o'er her shoulders waved like melted gold.
Around her next a heavenly mantle flowed,
That rich with Pallas' laboured colours glowed;
Large clasps of gold the foldings gathered round,
A golden zone her swelling bosom bound.   210
Far-beaming pendants tremble in her ear,
Each gem illumined with a triple star.
Then o'er her head she casts a veil more white
Than new-fall'n snow, and dazzling as the light.

Armed with the magic girdle of Venus, Juno joins Jove on Mount Ida. He is immediately seized with passion for her:

      'Let softer cares the present hour employ,
And be these moments sacred all to joy.
Ne'er did my soul so strong a passion prove,
Or for an earthly, or a heavenly love;   360
Not when I pressed Ixion's matchless dame,
Whence rose Perithous like the gods in fame;

Not when fair Danaë felt the shower of gold
Stream into life, whence Perseus brave and bold;
Not thus I burned for either Theban dame –   365
Bacchus from this, from that Alcides came –
Not Phoenix' daughter, beautiful and young,
Whence godlike Rhadamanth and Minos sprung;
Not thus I burned for fair Latona's face,
Nor comelier Ceres' more majestic grace;   370
Not thus ev'n for thyself I felt desire,
As now my veins receive the pleasing fire.'
        He spoke; the goddess with the charming eyes
Glows with celestial red, and thus replies:
'Is this a scene for love, on Ida's height,   375
Exposed to mortal and immortal sight?
Our joys profaned by each familiar eye,
The sport of heaven, and fable of the sky!
How shall I e'er review the blessed abodes,
Or mix among the Senate of the gods?   380
Shall I not think that, with disordered charms,
All heaven beholds me recent from thy arms?
With skill divine has Vulcan formed thy bower,
Sacred to love and to the genial hour;
If such thy will, to that recess retire,   385
And secret there indulge thy soft desire.'
        She ceased, and, smiling with superior love,
Thus answered mild the cloud-compelling Jove:
'Nor god, nor mortal shall our joys behold,
Shaded with clouds, and circumfused in gold,   390
Not ev'n the sun, who darts through heaven his rays,
And whose broad eye th' extended earth surveys.'
        Gazing he spoke, and, kindling at the view,
His eager arms around the goddess threw.
Glad Earth perceives, and from her bosom pours   395
Unbidden herbs and voluntary flowers;
Thick new-born violets a soft carpet spread,
And clustering lotus swelled the rising bed,
And sudden hyacinths the turf bestrow,
And flamy crocus made the mountain glow.   400
There golden clouds conceal the heavenly pair,
Steeped in soft joys, and circumfused with air;

Celestial dews, descending o'er the ground,
Perfume the mount, and breathe ambrosia round.
At length with love and sleep's soft power oppressed,   405
The panting Thunderer nods, and sinks to rest.

from **Book 15**

*In Jove's absence, Neptune seizes the opportunity to assist the Greeks
further. When Jove awakes and discovers the trick that has been
played on him, he angrily sends Iris to force Neptune to withdraw
from the fight. Jove is resolved that the Greeks' fortunes will not turn
until the firing of their ships. Hector is roused to lead a formidable
attack on the Greek army. Apollo assists in the breaching of the Greek
fortifications.*

The hosts rush on, loud clamours shake the shore;
The horses thunder, earth and ocean roar!   405
Apollo, planted at the trench's bound,
Pushed at the bank; down sunk th' enormous mound;
Rolled in the ditch the heapy ruin lay,
A sudden road, a long and ample way!
O'er the dread fosse, a late impervious space,   410
Now steeds, and men, and cars, tumultuous pass.
The wondering crowds the downward level trod;
Before them flamed the shield, and marched the god.
Then with his hand he shook the mighty wall;
And, lo, the turrets nod, the bulwarks fall!   415
Easy, as when ashore an infant stands,
And draws imagined houses in the sands;
The sportive wanton, pleased with some new play,
Sweeps the slight works and fashioned domes away:
Thus vanished, at thy touch, the towers and walls;   420
The toil of thousands in a moment falls!

Hector leads the Trojan advance on the ships.

So Mars, when human crimes for vengeance call,
Shakes his huge javelin, and whole armies fall.
Not with more rage a conflagration rolls,
Wraps the vast mountains, and involves the poles.
He foams with wrath; beneath his gloomy brow   730
Like fiery meteors his red eyeballs glow;
The radiant helmet on his temples burns,
Waves when he nods, and lightens as he turns:
For Jove his splendour round the chief had thrown,
And cast the blaze of both the hosts on one.   735
Unhappy glories! for his fate was near,
Due to stern Pallas, and Pelides' spear;
Yet Jove deferred the death he was to pay,
And gave what fate allowed, the honours of a day!
          Now all on fire for fame, his breast, his eyes   740
Burn at each foe, and single every prize;
Still at the closest ranks, the thickest fight,
He points his ardour, and exerts his might.
The Grecian phalanx, moveless as a tower,
On all sides battered, yet resists his power: 745
So some tall rock o'erhangs the hoary main,
By winds assailed, by billows beat in vain,
Unmoved it hears, above, the tempest blow,
And sees the watery mountains break below.
Girt in surrounding flames, he seems to fall   750
Like fire from Jove, and bursts upon them all;
Bursts as a wave that from the clouds impends,
And, swelled with tempests, on the ship descends;
White are the decks with foam; the winds aloud
Howl o'er the masts, and sing through every shroud: 755
Pale, trembling, tired, the sailors freeze with fears;
And instant death on every wave appears:
So pale the Greeks the eyes of Hector meet,
The chief so thunders, and so shakes the fleet.
          As when a lion, rushing from his den,   760
Amidst the plain of some wide-watered fen
(Where numerous oxen, as at ease they feed,
At large expatiate o'er the ranker mead),
Leaps on the herds before the herdsman's eyes;
The trembling herdsman far to distance flies: 765

Some lordly bull (the rest dispersed and fled)
He singles out, arrests, and lays him dead:
Thus from the rage of Jove-like Hector flew
All Greece in heaps.

from **Book 16**

*Seeing the Greeks in dire straits, Patroclus begs Achilles to relent and
return to the fight. Achilles refuses, but allows Patroclus to lead the
Myrmidons into battle, wearing his armour. Achilles himself musters
the Myrmidons for the fight.*

All breathing death, around their chief they stand,
A grim, terrific, formidable band:
Grim as voracious wolves that seek the springs
When scalding thirst their burning bowels wrings;   195
When some tall stag, fresh-slaughtered in the wood
Has drenched their wide, insatiate throats with blood;
To the black fount they rush, a hideous throng,
With paunch distended, and with lolling tongue,
Fire fills their eye, their black jaws belch the gore,   200
And gorged with slaughter, still they thirst for more:
Like furious, rushed the Myrmidonian crew,
Such their dread strength, and such their deathful view.

*Patroclus saves the Greek ships and leads a fierce attack on the Trojans.
As Jove had foreseen, Sarpedon attempts to stop his incursion.*

Jove viewed the combat, whose event foreseen,
He thus bespoke his sister and his queen:
'The hour draws on; the destinies ordain   530
My godlike son shall press the Phrygian plain.
Already on the verge of death he stands,
His life is owed to fierce Patroclus' hands.
What passions in a parent's breast debate!
Say, shall I snatch him from impending fate,   535

And send him safe to Lycia, distant far
From all the dangers and the toils of war,
Or to his doom my bravest offspring yield,
And fatten, with celestial blood, the field?'
      Then thus the goddess with the radiant eyes: 540
'What words are these, O sovereign of the skies?
Short is the date prescribed to mortal man;
Shall Jove for one extend the narrow span,
Whose bounds were fixed before his race began?
How many sons of gods, foredoomed to death,   545
Before proud Ilion, must resign their breath!
Were thine exempt, debate would rise above,
And murmuring powers condemn their partial Jove.
Give the bold chief a glorious fate in fight;
And when th' ascending soul has winged her flight,   550
Let Sleep and Death convey, by thy command,
The breathless body to his native land.
His friends and people, to his future praise,
A marble tomb and pyramid shall raise,
And lasting honours to his ashes give;   555
His fame – 'tis all the dead can have – shall live!'
      She said; the cloud-compeller, overcome,
Assents to fate, and ratifies the doom.
Then, touched with grief, the weeping heavens distilled
A shower of blood o'er all the fatal field.   560
The god, his eyes averting from the plain,
Laments his son, predestined to be slain,
Far from the Lycian shores, his happy native reign.

*Patroclus kills Sarpedon, and, ignoring Achilles' command and
Apollo's warning, presses on towards Troy.*

Then rash Patroclus with new fury glows,
And breathing slaughter, pours amid the foes.
Thrice on the press like Mars himself he flew,
And thrice three heroes at each onset slew.
There ends thy glory, there the fates untwine   950
The last, black remnant of so bright a line!
Apollo dreadful stops thy middle way;
Death calls, and heaven allows no longer day!

For lo! the god, in dusky clouds enshrined,
Approaching dealt a staggering blow behind.   955
The weighty shock his neck and shoulders feel;
His eyes flash sparkles, his stunned senses reel
In giddy darkness; far to distance flung,
His bounding helmet on the champain rung.
Achilles' plume is stained with dust and gore: 960
That plume, which never stooped to earth before,
Long used, untouched, in fighting fields to shine,
And shade the temples of the man divine.
Jove dooms it now on Hector's helm to nod;
Not long – for fate pursues him, and the god.   965
      His spear in shivers falls, his ample shield
Drops from his arm; his baldric strows the field;
The corselet his astonished breast forsakes;
Loose is each joint; each nerve with horror shakes.
Stupid he stares, and all-assistless stands: 970
Such is the force of more than mortal hands!
      A Dardan youth there was, well-known to fame,
From Panthus sprung, Euphorbus was his name;
Famed for the manage of the foaming horse,
Skilled in the dart, and matchless in the course: 975
Full twenty knights he tumbled from the car,
While yet he learned his rudiments of war.
His venturous spear first drew the hero's gore;
He struck, he wounded, but he durst no more;
Nor, though disarmed, Patroclus' fury stood,   980
But swift withdrew the long-protended wood,
And turned him short, and herded in the crowd.
Thus, by an arm divine, and mortal spear,
Wounded, at once, Patroclus yields to fear,
Retires for succour to his social train,   985
And flies the fate, which heaven decreed, in vain.
Stern Hector, as the bleeding chief he views,
Breaks through the ranks, and his retreat pursues;
The lance arrests him with a mortal wound;
He falls, earth thunders, and his arms resound.   990
With him all Greece was sunk; that moment all
Her yet-surviving heroes seemed to fall.
So scorched with heat, along the desert shore,

The roaming lion meets a bristly boar,
Fast by the spring; they both dispute the flood,   995
With flaming eyes, and jaws besmeared with blood;
At length the sovereign savage wins the strife,
And the torn boar resigns his thirst and life.
Patroclus thus, so many chiefs o'erthrown,
So many lives effused, expires his own.   1000
As dying now at Hector's feet he lies,
He sternly views him, and triumphing cries:
        'Lie there Patroclus, and with thee, the joy
Thy pride once promised, of subverting Troy!
The fancied scenes of Ilion wrapped in flames,   1005
And thy soft pleasures served with captive dames!
Unthinking man! I fought those towers to free,
And guard that beauteous race from lords like thee;
But thou a prey to vultures shalt be made!
Thy own Achilles cannot lend thee aid;   1010
Though much at parting that great chief might say,
And much enjoin thee, this important day.
"Return not, my brave friend," perhaps he said,
"Without the bloody arms of Hector dead."
He spoke, Patroclus marched, and thus he sped.'   1015
        Supine, and wildly gazing on the skies,
With faint, expiring breath the chief replies:
'Vain boaster, cease, and know the powers divine!
Jove's and Apollo's is this deed, not thine;
To heaven is owed whate'er your own you call,   1020
And heaven itself disarmed me ere my fall.
Had twenty mortals, each thy match in might,
Opposed me fairly, they had sunk in fight:
By fate and Phoebus was I first o'erthrown,
Euphorbus next; the third mean part thy own.   1025
But thou, imperious, hear my latest breath;
The gods inspire it, and it sounds thy death!
Insulting man, thou shalt be soon as I!
Black fate hangs o'er thee, and thy hour draws nigh;
Ev'n now on life's last verge I see thee stand,   1030
I see thee fall, and by Achilles' hand.'

from **Book 18**

News is brought to Achilles of Patroclus' death.

> A sudden horror shot through all the chief,   25
> And wrapped his senses in the cloud of grief;
> Cast on the ground, with furious hands he spread
> The scorching ashes o'er his graceful head;
> His purple garments, and his golden hairs,
> Those he deforms with dust, and these he tears: 30
> On the hard soil his groaning breast he threw,
> And rolled and grovelled, as to earth he grew.
> The virgin captives, with disordered charms
> (Won by his own, or by Patroclus' arms),
> Rushed from the tents with cries; and gathering round   35
> Beat their white breasts, and fainted on the ground,
> While Nestor's son sustains a manlier part,
> And mourns the warrior with a warrior's heart;
> Hangs on his arms, amidst his frantic woe,
> And oft prevents the meditated blow.   40

Achilles laments Patroclus' death, and declares to Thetis that he will kill Hector, even though his own death will follow shortly:

> 'Far lies Patroclus from his native plain!
> He fell, and, falling, wished my aid in vain.
> Ah then, since from this miserable day
> I cast all hope of my return away,   130
> Since, unrevenged, a hundred ghosts demand
> The fate of Hector from Achilles' hand,
> Since here, for brutal courage far renowned,
> I live an idle burden to the ground
> (Others in council famed for nobler skill,   135
> More useful to preserve, than I to kill),
> Let me – but oh, ye gracious powers above,
> Wrath and revenge from men and gods remove!
> Far, far too dear to every mortal breast,
> Sweet to the soul, as honey to the taste,   140
> Gathering like vapours of a noxious kind

From fiery blood, and darkening all the mind.
Me Agamemnon urged to deadly hate;
'Tis past – I quell it; I resign to fate.
Yes – I will meet the murderer of my friend,   145
Or, if the gods ordain it, meet my end.
The stroke of fate the bravest cannot shun:
The great Alcides, Jove's unequalled son,
To Juno's hate at length resigned his breath,
And sunk the victim of all-conquering death.   150
So shall Achilles fall, stretched pale and dead,
No more the Grecian hope, or Trojan dread!
Let me, this instant, rush into the fields,
And reap what glory life's short harvest yields.
Shall I not force some widowed dame to tear   155
With frantic hands her long, dishevelled hair?
Shall I not force her breast to heave with sighs,
And the soft tears to trickle from her eyes?
Yes, I shall give the fair those mournful charms –
In vain you hold me – hence! my arms, my arms –   160
Soon shall the sanguine torrent spread so wide,
That all shall know Achilles swells the tide.'

Achilles' blazing presence on the ramparts, and his mighty war-cry,
fill the Trojans with dreadful foreboding.

                              The hero rose;
Her aegis Pallas o'er his shoulder throws,
Around his brows a golden cloud she spread;
A stream of glory flamed above his head.
As when from some beleaguered town arise   245
The smokes high curling to the shaded skies
(Seen from some island o'er the main afar,
When men distressed hang out the sign of war);
Soon as the sun in ocean hides his rays,
Thick on the hills the flaming beacons blaze;   250
With long-projected beams the seas are bright,
And heaven's high arch reflects the ruddy light:
So from Achilles' head the splendours rise,
Reflecting blaze on blaze against the skies.
Forth marched the chief, and, distant from the crowd,   255

High on the rampart raised his voice aloud;
With her own shout Minerva swells the sound;
Troy starts astonished, and the shores rebound.
As the loud trumpet's brazen mouth from far
With shrilling clangour sounds th' alarm of war,   260
Struck from the walls, the echoes float on high,
And the round bulwarks and thick towers reply:
So high his brazen voice the hero reared,
Hosts dropped their arms, and trembled as they heard;
And back the chariots roll, and coursers bound,   265
And steeds and men lie mingled on the ground.
Aghast they see the living lightnings play,
And turn their eyeballs from the flashing ray.
Thrice from the trench his dreadful voice he raised;
And thrice they fled, confounded and amazed.   270

*At Thetis' request, Vulcan forges arms for Achilles. Achilles' shield is
decorated with pictures of the various regions of heaven and earth, and
the different activities of mankind, including the life of countrymen.*

Another field rose high with waving grain;
With bended sickles stand the reaper train.
Here stretched in ranks the levelled swarths are found,
Sheaves heaped on sheaves here thicken up the ground.   640
With sweeping stroke the mowers strew the lands;
The gatherers follow, and collect in bands;
And last the children, in whose arms are borne
(Too short to gripe them) the brown sheaves of corn.
The rustic monarch of the field descries   645
With silent glee the heaps around him rise.
A ready banquet on the turf is laid,
Beneath an ample oak's expanded shade.
The victim ox the sturdy youth prepare;
The reaper's due repast, the women's care.   650
Next, ripe in yellow gold, a vineyard shines,
Bent with the ponderous harvest of its vines;
A deeper dye the dangling clusters show,
And curled on silver props in order glow:
A darker metal mixed intrenched the place;   655
And pales of glittering tin th' enclosure grace.

To this, one pathway gently winding leads,
Where march a train with baskets on their heads,
Fair maids, and blooming youths, that smiling bear
The purple product of th' autumnal year.   660
To these a youth awakes the warbling strings,
Whose tender lay the fate of Linus sings;
In measured dance behind him move the train,
Tune soft the voice, and answer to the strain.

from **Book 19**

*At a council of the Greeks, Achilles renounces his wrath, and is
reconciled with Agamemnon. Briseis is returned to Achilles. Achilles
processes forth for battle, dressed in the armour made for him by
Vulcan.*

Now issued from the ships the warrior train,
And like a deluge poured upon the plain;
As when the piercing blasts of Boreas blow,   380
And scatter o'er the fields the driving snow;
From dusky clouds the fleecy winter flies,
Whose dazzling lustre whitens all the skies:
So helms succeeding helms, so shields from shields
Catch the quick beams, and brighten all the fields;   385
Broad-glittering breastplates, spears with pointed rays
Mix in one stream, reflecting blaze on blaze.
Thick beats the centre as the coursers bound,
With splendour flame the skies, and laugh the fields around.
Full in the midst, high towering o'er the rest,   390
His limbs in arms divine Achilles dressed;
Arms which the father of the fire bestowed,
Forged on th' eternal anvils of the god.
Grief and revenge his furious heart inspire,
His glowing eyeballs roll with living fire,   395
He grinds his teeth, and furious with delay
O'erlooks th' embattled host, and hopes the bloody day.

The silver cuishes first his thighs infold;
Then o'er his breast was braced the hollow gold:
The brazen sword a various baldric tied,   400
That, starred with gems, hung glittering at his side;
And, like the moon, the broad refulgent shield
Blazed with long rays, and gleamed athwart the field.
    So to night-wandering sailors, pale with fears,
Wide o'er the watery waste a light appears,   405
Which on the far-seen mountain blazing high
Streams from some lonely watch-tower to the sky;
With mournful eyes they gaze, and gaze again,
Loud howls the storm, and drives them o'er the main.
    Next, his high head the helmet graced; behind   410
The sweepy crest hung floating in the wind:
Like the red star, that from his flaming hair
Shakes down diseases, pestilence and war:
So streamed the golden honours from his head,
Trembled the sparkling plumes, and the loose glories shed. 415
    The chief beholds himself with wondering eyes;
His arms he poises, and his motions tries;
Buoyed by some inward force, he seems to swim,
And feels a pinion lifting every limb.
    And now he shakes his great paternal spear,   420
Ponderous and huge, which not a Greek could rear.
From Pelion's cloudy top an ash entire
Old Chiron felled, and shaped it for his sire;
A spear which stern Achilles only wields,
The death of heroes, and the dread of fields.   425
    Automedon and Alcimus prepare
Th' immortal coursers, and the radiant car
(The silver traces sweeping at their side),
Their fiery mouths resplendent bridles tied,
The iv'ry-studded reins, returned behind,   430
Waved o'er their backs, and to the chariot joined.
The charioteer then whirled the lash around,
And swift ascended at one active bound.
All bright in heavenly arms, above his squire
Achilles mounts, and sets the field on fire;   435
Not brighter Phoebus in th' ethereal way
Flames from his chariot, and restores the day.

High o'er the host, all terrible he stands,
And thunders to his steeds these dread commands:
      'Xanthus and Balius, of Podarge's strain,   440
(Unless ye boast that heavenly race in vain)
Be swift, be mindful of the load ye bear,
And learn to make your master more your care!
Through falling squadrons bear my slaughtering sword,
Nor, as ye left Patroclus, leave your lord.'   445
      The generous Xanthus, as the words he said,
Seemed sensible of woe, and drooped his head;
Trembling he stood before the golden wain,
And bowed to dust the honours of his mane;
When, strange to tell – so Juno willed – he broke   450
Eternal silence, and portentous spoke:
'Achilles, yes, this day at least we bear
Thy rage in safety through the files of war;
But come it will, the fatal time must come,
Nor ours the fault, but God decrees thy doom.   455
Not through our crime, or slowness in the course,
Fell thy Patroclus, but by heavenly force.
The bright, far-shooting god who gilds the day –
Confessed we saw him – tore his arms away.
No – could our swiftness o'er the winds prevail,   460
Or beat the pinions of the western gale,
All were in vain – the Fates thy death demand,
Due to a mortal and immortal hand.'
      Then ceased for ever, by the Furies tied,
His fateful voice. Th' intrepid chief replied   465
With unabated rage: 'So let it be!
Portents and prodigies are lost on me.
I know my fate: to die, to see no more
My much loved parents, and my native shore –
Enough – when heaven ordains, I sink in night,   470
Now perish Troy!' He said, and rushed to fight.

from **Book 20**

Achilles re-enters the battle and pursues the Trojans, committing great slaughter.

As when a flame the winding valley fills,
And runs on crackling shrubs between the hills;   570
Then o'er the stubble up the mountain flies,
Fires the high woods, and blazes to the skies,
This way and that the spreading torrent roars:
So sweeps the hero through the wasted shores;
Around him wide, immense destruction pours,   575
And earth is deluged with the sanguine showers.
As with autumnal harvests covered o'er,
And thick bestrewn, lies Ceres' sacred floor,
When round and round, with never-wearied pain,
The trampling steers beat out th' unnumbered grain: 580
So the fierce coursers, as the chariot rolls,
Tread down whole ranks, and crush out heroes' souls.
Dashed from their hoofs while o'er the dead they fly,
Black bloody drops the smoking chariot dye,
The spiky wheels through heaps of carnage tore,   585
And thick the groaning axles dropped with gore.
High o'er the scene of death Achilles stood,
All grim with dust, all horrible in blood,
Yet still insatiate, still with rage on flame:
Such is the lust of never-dying fame!

from **Book 21**

Achilles kills Priam's young son, Lycaon.

Then, as once more he plunged amid the flood,   40
The young Lycaon in his passage stood,
The son of Priam, whom the hero's hand

But late made captive in his father's land
(As from a sycamore his sounding steel
Lopped the green arms to spoke a chariot wheel);⁣ 45
To Lemnos' isle he sold the royal slave,
Where Jason's son the price demanded gave;
But kind Eëtion touching on the shore
The ransomed prince to fair Arisbè bore.
Ten days were past, since in his father's reign 50
He felt the sweets of liberty again;
The next, that god, whom men in vain withstand,
Gives the same youth to the same conquering hand;
Now never to return! and doomed to go
A sadder journey to the shades below. 55
His well-known face when great Achilles eyed
(The helm and visor he had cast aside
With wild affright, and dropped upon the field
His useless lance and unavailing shield),
As trembling, panting, from the stream he fled, 60
And knocked his faltering knees, the hero said:
⁣   'Ye mighty gods! What wonders strike my view:
Is it in vain our conquering arms subdue?
Sure I shall see yon heaps of Trojans killed
Rise from the shades, and brave me on the field; 65
As now the captive, whom so late I bound
And sold to Lemnos, stalks on Trojan ground!
Not him the seas unmeasured deeps detain,
That bar such numbers from their native plain.
Lo, he returns! Try then, my flying spear, 70
Try, if the grave can hold the wanderer;
If earth at length this active prince can seize,
Earth, whose strong grasp has held down Hercules!'
⁣   Thus while he spake, the Trojan pale with fears
Approached, and sought his knees with suppliant tears; 75
Loth as he was to yield his youthful breath,
And his soul shivering at th' approach of death.
Achilles raised the spear, prepared to wound;
He kissed his feet, extended on the ground;
And while above the spear suspended stood, 80
Longing to dip its thirsty point in blood,
One hand embraced them close, one stopped the dart,

While thus these melting words attempt his heart:
　　　'Thy well-known captive, great Achilles, see,
Once more Lycaon trembles at thy knee!   85
Some pity to a suppliant's name afford,
Who shared the gifts of Ceres at thy board,
Whom late thy conquering arm to Lemnos bore,
Far from his father, friends, and native shore;
A hundred oxen were his price that day,   90
Now sums immense thy mercy shall repay.
Scarce respited from woes I yet appear,
And scarce twelve morning suns have seen me here;
Lo! Jove again submits me to thy hands,
Again, her victim cruel fate demands!   95
I sprung from Priam, and Laothoë fair
(Old Altes' daughter, and Lelegia's heir;
Who held in Pedasus his famed abode,
And ruled the fields where silver Satnio flowed);
Two sons – alas, unhappy sons! – she bore,   100
For, ah, one spear shall drink each brother's gore,
And I succeed to slaughtered Polydore!
How from that arm of terror shall I fly?
Some demon urges! 'Tis my doom to die!
If ever yet soft pity touched thy mind,   105
Ah, think not me too much of Hector's kind!
Not the same mother gave thy suppliant breath,
With his, who wrought thy loved Patroclus' death.'
　　　　　These words, attended with a shower of tears,
The youth addressed to unrelenting ears.   110
'Talk not of life, or ransom,' he replies,
'Patroclus dead, whoever meets me, dies,
In vain a single Trojan sues for grace,
But least, the sons of Priam's hateful race.
Die then, my friend! What boots it to deplore?   115
The great, the good Patroclus is no more!
He, far thy better, was fore-doomed to die,
And thou, dost thou bewail mortality?
See'st thou not me, whom nature's gifts adorn,
Sprung from a hero, from a goddess born?   120
The day shall come – which nothing can avert –
When by the spear, the arrow, or the dart,

By night, or day, by force, or by design,
Impending death and certain fate are mine!
Die then!' He said; and as the word he spoke   125
The fainting stripling sunk before the stroke,
His hand forgot its grasp, and left the spear,
While all his trembling frame confessed his fear.
Sudden, Achilles his broad sword displayed,
And buried in his neck the reeking blade.   130
Prone fell the youth; and panting on the land,
The gushing purple dyed the thirsty sand;
The victor to the stream the carcass gave,
And thus insults him, floating on the wave:

     'Lie there, Lycaon! let the fish surround   135
Thy bloated corse, and suck thy gory wound:
There no sad mother shall thy funerals weep,
But swift Scamander roll thee to the deep,
Whose every wave some watery monster brings,
To feast unpunished on the fat of kings.   140
So perish Troy, and all the Trojan line!
Such ruin theirs, and such compassion mine.
What boots ye now Scamander's worshipped stream,
His earthly honours, and immortal name?
In vain your immolated bulls are slain,   145
Your living coursers glut his gulfs in vain;
Thus he rewards you, with this bitter fate,
Thus, till the Grecian vengeance is complete;
Thus is atoned Patroclus' honoured shade,
And the short absence of Achilles paid.'   150

*The river Scamander, enraged at the choking of his streams by the
corpses of warriors slain by Achilles, attacks the hero.*

Then rising in his rage above the shores,
From all his deep the bellowing river roars,
Huge heaps of slain disgorges on the coast,
And round the banks the ghastly dead are tossed.   260
While all before, the billows ranged on high
(A watery bulwark) screen the bands who fly.
Now bursting on his head with thundering sound,
The falling deluge whelms the hero round:

His loaded shield bends to the rushing tide;   265
His feet, upborne, scarce the strong flood divide,
Sliddering, and staggering. On the border stood
A spreading elm, that overhung the flood;
He seized a bending bough, his steps to stay;
The plant uprooted to his weight gave way,   270
Heaving the bank, and undermining all;
Loud flash the waters to the rushing fall
Of the thick foliage. The large trunk displayed
Bridged the rough flood across; the hero stayed
On this his weight, and, raised upon his hand,   275
Leapt from the channel, and regained the land.
Then blackened the wild waves; the murmur rose;
The god pursues, a huger billow throws,
And bursts the bank, ambitious to destroy
The man whose fury is the fate of Troy.   280
He, like the warlike eagle speeds his pace
(Swiftest and strongest of th' aërial race);
Far as a spear can fly, Achilles springs;
At every bound his clanging armour rings.
Now here, now there, he turns on every side,   285
And winds his course before the following tide;
The waves flow after, wheresoe'er he wheels,
And gather fast, and murmur at his heels;
So when a peasant to his garden brings
Soft rills of water from the bubbling springs,   290
And calls the floods from high, to bless his bowers
And feed with pregnant streams the plants and flowers;
Soon as he clears whate'er their passage stayed,
And marks the future current with his spade,
Swift o'er the rolling pebbles, down the hills,   295
Louder and louder purl the falling rills,
Before him scattering, they prevent his pains,
And shine in mazy wanderings o'er the plains.
          Still flies Achilles, but before his eyes
Still swift Scamander rolls where'er he flies;   300
Not all his speed escapes the rapid floods,
The first of men, but not a match for gods.
Oft as he turned, the torrent to oppose,

And bravely try if all the powers were foes;
So oft the surge, in watery mountains spread,   305
Beats on his back, or bursts upon his head.
Yet dauntless still the adverse flood he braves,
And still indignant bounds above the waves.
Tired by the tides, his knees relax with toil;
Washed from beneath him slides the slimy soil.   310

from **Book 22**

*Despite Priam's and Hecuba's pleas that he should withdraw within
the city walls, Hector awaits Achilles' attack. He meditates on the
moment of crisis:*

'Where lies my way? To enter in the wall?
Honour and shame th' ungenerous thought recall:
Shall proud Polydamas before the gate   140
Proclaim his counsels are obeyed too late,
Which, timely followed but the former night,
What numbers had been saved by Hector's flight?
That wise advice rejected with disdain,
I feel my folly in my people slain.   145
Methinks my suffering country's voice I hear,
But most, her worthless sons insult my ear,
On my rash courage charge the chance of war,
And blame those virtues which they cannot share.
No, if I e'er return, return I must   150
Glorious, my country's terror laid in dust;
Or if I perish, let her see me fall
In field at least, and fighting for her wall.
And yet suppose these measures I forego,
Approach unarmed, and parley with the foe,   155
The warrior-shield, the helm, and lance lay down,
And treat on terms of peace to save the town:
The wife withheld, the treasure ill detained
(Cause of the war, and grievance of the land),

With honourable justice to restore;   160
And add half Ilion's yet remaining store,
Which Troy shall, sworn, produce, that injured Greece
May share our wealth, and leave our walls in peace.
But why this thought? Unarmed if I should go,
What hope of mercy from this vengeful foe?   165
But woman-like to fall, and fall without a blow?
We greet not here, as man conversing man
Met at an oak, or journeying o'er a plain;
No season now for calm familiar talk,
Like youths and maidens in an evening walk: 170
War is our business, but to whom is given
To die or triumph, that determine heaven!'
      Thus pondering, like a god the Greek drew nigh;
His dreadful plumage nodded from on high;
The Pelian javelin, in his better hand,   175
Shot trembling rays that glittered o'er the land;
And on his breast the beamy splendours shone
Like Jove's own lightning, or the rising sun.
As Hector sees, unusual terrors rise,
Struck by some god, he fears, recedes, and flies.   180
He leaves the gates, he leaves the walls behind;
Achilles follows like the wingèd wind.
Thus at the panting dove a falcon flies
(The swiftest racer of the liquid skies),
Just when he holds, or thinks he holds, his prey,   185
Obliquely wheeling through th' aërial way;
With open beak and shrilling cries he springs,
And aims his claws, and shoots upon his wings:
No less foreright the rapid chase they held,
One urged by fury, one by fear impelled;   190
Now circling round the walls their course maintain,
Where the high watch-tower overlooks the plain,
Now where the fig-trees spread their umbrage broad –
A wider compass – smoke along the road.
Next by Scamander's double source they bound,   195
Where two famed fountains burst the parted ground;
This hot through scorching clefts is seen to rise,
With exhalations steaming to the skies;
That the green banks in summer's heat o'erflows,

Like crystal clear, and cold as winter-snows;   200
Each gushing fount a marble cistern fills,
Whose polished bed receives the falling rills,
Where Trojan dames, ere yet alarmed by Greece,
Washed their fair garments in the days of peace.
By these they passed, one chasing, one in flight   205
(The mighty fled, pursued by stronger might);
Swift was the course; no vulgar prize they play,
No vulgar victim must reward the day,
Such as in races crown the speedy strife:
The prize contended was great Hector's life.   210

Jove weighs the fates of the two heroes.

Jove lifts the golden balances, that show
The fates of mortal men and things below:
Here each contending hero's lot he tries,
And weighs, with equal hand, their destinies.
Low sinks the scale surcharged with Hector's fate;   275
Heavy with death it sinks, and hell receives the weight.

After an exchange of javelin-throws, Hector charges at Achilles.

Fierce, at the word, his weighty sword he drew
And, all collected, on Achilles flew.   390
So Jove's bold bird, high-balanced in the air,
Stoops from the clouds to truss the quivering hare.
Nor less Achilles his fierce soul prepares;
Before his breast the flaming shield he bears,
Refulgent orb! Above his four-fold cone   395
The gilded horsehair sparkled in the sun,
Nodding at every step (Vulcanian frame!),
And as he moved, his figure seemed on flame.
As radiant Hesper shines with keener light,
Far-beaming o'er the silver host of night,   400
When all the starry train emblaze the sphere:
So shone the point of great Achilles' spear.
In his right hand he waves the weapon round,
Eyes the whole man, and meditates the wound;
But the rich mail Patroclus lately wore,   405

Securely cased the warrior's body o'er.
One place at length he spies, to let in fate,
Where 'twixt the neck and throat the jointed plate
Gave entrance: through that penetrable part
Furious he drove the well-directed dart;   410
Nor pierced the windpipe yet, nor took the power
Of speech, unhappy, from thy dying hour!
Prone on the field the bleeding warrior lies,
While, thus triumphing, stern Achilles cries:

  'At last is Hector stretched upon the plain,   415
Who feared no vengeance for Patroclus slain:
Then, prince, you should have feared what now you feel!
Achilles absent was Achilles still.
Yet a short space the great avenger stayed,
Then low in dust thy strength and glory laid.   420
Peaceful he sleeps, with all our rites adorned,
For ever honoured, and for ever mourned,
While, cast to all the rage of hostile power,
Thee birds shall mangle, and the dogs devour!'

  Then Hector, fainting at th' approach of death: 425
'By thy own soul, by those who gave thee breath,
By all the sacred prevalence of prayer,
Ah, leave me not for Grecian dogs to tear!
The common rites of sepulture bestow,
To soothe a father's and a mother's woe;   430
Let their large gifts procure an urn at least,
And Hector's ashes in his country rest.'

  'No, wretch accursed!' relentless he replies
(Flames, as he spoke, shot flashing from his eyes),
'Not those who gave me breath should bid me spare,   435
Nor all the sacred prevalence of prayer.
Could I myself the bloody banquet join!
No – to the dogs that carcass I resign.
Should Troy, to bribe me, bring forth all her store,
And giving thousands, offer thousands more;   440
Should Dardan Priam, and the weeping dame,
Drain their whole realm to buy one funeral flame;
Their Hector on the pile they should not see,
Nor rob the vultures of one limb of thee!'

  Then thus the chief his dying accents drew: 445

'Thy rage, implacable, too well I knew:
The Furies that relentless breast have steeled,
And cursed thee with a heart that cannot yield.
Yet think, a day will come, when fate's decree
And angry gods shall wreak this wrong on thee;   450
Phoebus and Paris shall avenge my fate,
And stretch thee here, before this Scaean gate.'
          He ceased. The fates suppressed his labouring breath,
And his eyes stiffened at the hand of death;
To the dark realm the spirit wings its way   455
(The manly body left a load of clay),
And plaintive glides along the dreary coast,
A naked, wandering, melancholy ghost!

Achilles strips Hector's body and subjects it to further indignity.

          Then his fell soul a thought of vengeance bred   495
(Unworthy of himself, and of the dead),
The nervous ankles bored, his feet he bound
With thongs inserted through the double wound;
These fixed up high behind the rolling wain,
His graceful head was trailed along the plain.   500
Proud on his car th' insulting victor stood,
And bore aloft his arms, distilling blood.
He smites the steeds, the rapid chariot flies,
The sudden clouds of circling dust arise.
Now lost is all that formidable air;   505
The face divine, and long-descending hair
Purple the ground, and streak the sable sand;
Deformed, dishonoured, in his native land,
Giv'n to the rage of an insulting throng,
And, in his parent's sight, now dragged along!   510

from **Book 23**

That night, the ghost of Patroclus appears to Achilles.

In the same robe he living wore, he came,   80
In stature, voice, and pleasing look, the same.
The form familiar hovered o'er his head,
          'And sleeps Achilles,' thus the phantom said,
'Sleeps my Achilles, his Patroclus dead?
Living, I seemed his dearest, tenderest care,   85
But, now forgot, I wander in the air.
Let my pale corse the rites of burial know,
And give me entrance in the realms below;
Till then, the spirit finds no resting place,
But here and there th' unbodied spectres chase   90
The vagrant dead around the dark abode,
Forbid to cross th' irremeable flood.
Now give thy hand; for to the farther shore
When once we pass, the soul returns no more.
When once the last funereal flames ascend,   95
No more shall meet Achilles and his friend,
No more our thoughts to those we loved make known,
Or quit the dearest, to converse alone.
Me fate has severed from the sons of earth,
The fate foredoomed that waited from my birth,   100
Thee too it waits; before the Trojan wall
Ev'n great and god-like thou art doomed to fall.
Hear then; and as in fate and love we join,
Ah, suffer that my bones may rest with thine!
Together have we lived, together bred,   105
One house received us, and one table fed;
That golden urn thy goddess mother gave
May mix our ashes in one common grave.'

from **Book 24**

Apollo protests to the other gods at Achilles' excesses. Thetis, at Jove's command, orders Achilles to cease his wrath, and return Hector's body to his family. Iris is sent by Jove to instruct Priam to visit Achilles and ransom Hector's remains. With Hermes' protection, Priam journeys to Achilles' tent, and, prostrating himself before the hero, makes his request:

'Ah think, thou favoured of the powers divine!
Think of thy father's age, and pity mine!
In me, that father's reverend image trace,   600
Those silver hairs, that venerable face;
His trembling limbs, his helpless person, see,
In all my equal, but in misery!
Yet now, perhaps, some turn of human fate
Expels him helpless from his peaceful state;   605
Think from some powerful foe thou see'st him fly,
And beg protection with a feeble cry.
Yet still one comfort in his soul may rise –
He hears his son still lives to glad his eyes;
And, hearing, still may hope a better day   610
May send him thee, to chase that foe away.
No comfort to my griefs, no hopes remain,
The best, the bravest of my sons are slain!
Yet what a race! Ere Greece to Ilion came,
The pledge of many a loved and loving dame;   615
Nineteen one mother bore – dead, all are dead!
How oft, alas, has wretched Priam bled!
Still one was left, their loss to recompense,
His father's hope, his country's last defence.
Him too thy rage has slain! Beneath thy steel,   620
Unhappy, in his country's cause he fell!
     For him, through hostile camps I bent my way,
For him thus prostrate at thy feet I lay;
Large gifts, proportioned to thy wrath, I bear;
Oh hear the wretched, and the gods revere!   625
     Think of thy father, and this face behold!
See him in me, as helpless and as old!

Though not so wretched: there he yields to me,
The first of men in sovereign misery!
Thus forced to kneel, thus grovelling to embrace   630
The scourge and ruin of my realm and race,
Suppliant my children's murderer to implore,
And kiss those hands yet reeking with their gore!'
    These words soft pity in the chief inspire,
Touched with the dear remembrance of his sire.   635
Then with his hand, as prostrate still he lay,
The old man's cheek he gently turned away.
Now each by turns indulged the gush of woe,
And now the mingled tides together flow;
This low on earth, that gently bending o'er,   640
A father one, and one a son, deplore;
But great Achilles different passions rend,
And now his sire he mourns, and now his friend.
Th' infectious softness through the heroes ran;
One universal, solemn shower began;   645
They bore as heroes, but they felt as man.
    Satiate at length with unavailing woes
From the high throne divine Achilles rose;
The reverend monarch by the hand he raised;
On his white beard and form majestic gazed,   650
Not unrelenting; then serene began
With words to sooth the miserable man:
    'Alas, what weight of anguish hast thou known,
Unhappy prince, thus guardless and alone
To pass through foes, and thus undaunted face   655
The man whose fury has destroyed thy race!
Heaven sure has armed thee with a heart of steel,
A strength proportioned to the woes you feel.
Rise then: let reason mitigate our care:
To mourn, avails not: man is born to bear.   660
Such is, alas, the gods' severe decree;
They, only they are blessed, and only free!
Two urns by Jove's high throne have ever stood,
The source of evil one, and one of good;
From thence the cup of mortal man he fills,   665
Blessings to these, to those distributes ills;
To most, he mingles both: the wretch decreed

To taste the bad, unmixed, is cursed indeed;
Pursued by wrongs, by meagre famine driven,
He wanders, outcast both of earth and heaven.   670
The happiest taste not happiness sincere,
But find the cordial draught is dashed with care.
Who more than Peleus shone in wealth and power?
What stars concurring blessed his natal hour!
A realm, a goddess, to his wishes given,   675
Graced by the gods with all the gifts of heaven!
One evil yet o'ertakes his latest day:
No race succeeding to imperial sway;
An only son, and he, alas, ordained
To fall untimely in a foreign land!   680
See him, in Troy, the pious care decline
Of his weak age, to live the curse of thine!
Thou too, old man, hast happier days beheld,
In riches once, in children once excelled;
Extended Phrygia owned thy ample reign,   685
And all fair Lesbos' blissful seats contain,
And all wide Hellespont's unmeasured main.
But since the god his hand has pleased to turn,
And fill thy measure from his bitter urn,
What sees the sun, but hapless heroes' falls?   690
War and the blood of men surround thy walls!
What must be, must be. Bear thy lot, nor shed
These unavailing sorrows o'er the dead;
Thou can'st not call him from the Stygian shore,
But thou, alas, may'st live, to suffer more!'   695
         To whom the king: 'O favoured of the skies,
Here let me grow to earth, since Hector lies
On the bare beach, deprived of obsequies!
Oh give me Hector! To my eyes restore
His corse, and take the gifts: I ask no more.   700
Thou, as thou may'st, these boundless stores enjoy,
Safe may'st thou sail, and turn thy wrath from Troy;
So shall thy pity and forbearance give
A weak old man to see the light and live!'
         'Move me no more,' Achilles thus replies,   705
While kindling anger sparkled in his eyes,
'Nor seek by tears my steady soul to bend;

To yield thy Hector I myself intend:
For know, from Jove my goddess-mother came
(Old Ocean's daughter, silver-footed dame),   710
Nor com'st thou but by heaven, nor com'st alone:
Some god impels with courage not thy own;
No human hand the weighty gates unbarred,
Nor could the boldest of our youth have dared
To pass our outworks, or elude the guard.   715
Cease, lest neglectful of high Jove's command
I show thee, king, thou tread'st on hostile land!
Release my knees, thy suppliant arts give o'er,
And shake the purpose of my soul no more!'

Priam returns to Troy with Hector's body. Andromache laments her dead husband.

First to the corse the weeping consort flew,
Around his neck her milk-white arms she threw,
And, 'O, my Hector! O, my lord!' she cries,
'Snatched in thy bloom from these desiring eyes!
Thou to the dismal realms for ever gone!   910
And I abandoned, desolate, alone!
An only son, once comfort of our pains,
Sad product now of hapless love, remains!
Never to manly age that son shall rise,
Or with increasing graces glad my eyes: 915
For Ilion now, her great defender slain,
Shall sink, a smoking ruin on the plain.
Who now protects her wives with guardian care?
Who saves her infants from the rage of war?
Now hostile fleets must waft those infants o'er –   920
Those wives must wait 'em – to a foreign shore!
Thou too, my son, to barbarous climes shalt go,
The sad companion of thy mother's woe!
Driv'n hence a slave before the victor's sword;
Condemned to toil for some inhuman lord.   925
Or else some Greek whose father pressed the plain,
Or son, or brother, by great Hector slain,
In Hector's blood his vengeance shall enjoy,
And hurl thee headlong from the towers of Troy.

For thy stern father never spared a foe: 930
Thence all these tears, and all this scene of woe!
Thence many evils his sad parents bore,
His parents many, but his consort more.
Why gav'st thou not to me thy dying hand?
And why received not I thy last command?   935
Some word thou would'st have spoke, which sadly dear,
My soul might keep, or utter with a tear;
Which never, never could be lost in air,
Fixed in my heart, and oft repeated there!'

*The Trojans mourn Hector for nine days. On the tenth day, his
monument is raised, and the eleventh is spent in solemn feasting. On
the twelfth day, Priam has told Achilles, the battle will recommence.*

from **The Odyssey**

from **Book 1**

Homer's subject: the wanderings and homecoming of Ulysses.

The man, for wisdom's various arts renowned,
Long exercised in woes, O Muse, resound!
Who, when his arms had wrought the destined fall
Of sacred Troy, and razed her heaven-built wall,
Wandering from clime to clime, observant strayed,   5
Their manners noted, and their states surveyed.
On stormy seas unnumbered toils he bore,
Safe with his friends to gain his natal shore:
Vain toils! Their impious folly dared to prey
On herds devoted to the god of day;   10
The god vindictive doomed them never more
(Ah, men unblessed!) to touch that natal shore.
Oh snatch some portion of these acts from fate,
Celestial Muse, and to our world relate!

While Ulysses is detained on Calypso's island, his palace in Ithaca is besieged by suitors for the hand of his faithful wife, Penelope. Minerva, disguised as Mentes, appears to Ulysses' son, Telemachus, and advises him to voyage in search of news of his father.

from **Book 2**

*Telemachus summons a council of the lords of Ithaca, and complains
about the suitors' behaviour. Antinoüs, the most arrogant of the
suitors, complains at Telemachus' impudence, and Penelope's deceit:*

        'O insolence of youth, whose tongue affords   95
Such railing eloquence, and war of words!
Studious thy country's worthies to defame,
Thy erring voice displays thy mother's shame.
Elusive of the bridal day, she gives
Fond hopes to all, and all with hopes deceives.   100
Did not the sun, through heaven's wide azure rolled,
For three long years the royal fraud behold?
While she, laborious in delusion, spread
The spacious loom, and mixed the various thread;
Where as to life the wondrous figures rise,   105
Thus spoke th' inventive queen, with artful sighs:
        "Though cold in death Ulysses breathes no more,
Cease yet a while to urge the bridal hour;
Cease, till to great Laertes I bequeath
A task of grief, his ornaments of death;   110
Lest when the fates his royal ashes claim,
The Grecian matrons taint my spotless fame,
When he, whom living mighty realms obeyed,
Shall want in death a shroud to grace his shade."
        Thus she; at once the generous train complies,   115
Nor fraud mistrusts in virtue's fair disguise.
The work she plied; but, studious of delay,
By night reversed the labours of the day.
While thrice the sun his annual journey made,
The conscious lamp the midnight fraud surveyed;   120
Unheard, unseen, three years her arts prevail;
The fourth, her maid unfolds th' amazing tale.
We saw, as unperceived we took our stand,
The backward labours of her faithless hand.
Then urged, she perfects her illustrious toils;   125
A wondrous monument of female wiles!'

*Telemachus, assisted by Minerva (now disguised as Mentor) embarks
on his voyage. He visits Nestor and Menelaus, who tell him of the fate*

*of the returning Greeks, and of Ulysses' exploits at Troy: Menelaus
has heard that Ulysses is currently being detained against his will by
Calypso.*

from **Book 5**

Jove sends Hermes to order Calypso to release Ulysses.

Large was the grot in which the nymph he found
(The fair-haired nymph with every beauty crowned);
She sat and sung, the rocks resound her lays;
The cave was brightened with a rising blaze;   75
Cedar and frankincense, an odorous pile,
Flamed on the hearth, and wide perfumed the isle,
While she with work and song the time divides,
And through the loom the golden shuttle guides;
Without the grot, a various sylvan scene   80
Appeared around, and groves of living green;
Poplars and alders ever quivering played,
And nodding cypress formed a fragrant shade;
On whose high branches, waving with the storm,
The birds of broadest wing their mansion form,   85
The chough, the sea-mew, the loquacious crow,
And scream aloft, and skim the deeps below.
Depending vines the shelving cavern screen,
With purple clusters blushing through the green.
Four limpid fountains from the clefts distil,   90
And every fountain pours a several rill,
In mazy windings wandering down the hill,
Where bloomy meads with virid greens were crowned,
And glowing violets threw odours round.
A scene, where if a god should cast his sight,   95
A god might gaze, and wander with delight!
Joy touched the messenger of heaven; he stayed

Entranced, and all the blissful haunt surveyed.
Him, entering in the cave, Calypso knew,
For powers celestial to each other's view   100
Stand still confessed, though distant far they lie
To habitants of earth, or sea, or sky.
But sad Ulysses, by himself apart,
Poured the big sorrows of his swelling heart;
All on the lonely shore he sat to weep,   105
And rolled his eyes around the restless deep;
Toward his loved coast he rolled his eyes in vain,
Till dimmed with rising grief, they streamed again.

Calypso sadly accedes to the god's request, and advises Ulysses to build
a raft. At their last meal together, she laments his departure.

  'Ulysses!' with a sigh she thus began,
'O sprung from gods, in wisdom more than man!
Is then thy home the passion of thy heart?
Thus wilt thou leave me? Are we thus to part?   260
Farewell, and ever joyful may'st thou be,
Nor break the transport with one thought of me!
But ah, Ulysses, wert thou giv'n to know
What fate yet dooms thee, yet, to undergo,
Thy heart might settle in this scene of ease,   265
And ev'n these slighted charms might learn to please!
A willing goddess, and immortal life,
Might banish from thy mind an absent wife.
Am I inferior to a mortal dame?
Less soft my feature, less august my frame?   270
Or shall the daughters of mankind compare
Their earth-born beauties with the heavenly fair?'
  'Alas, for this!' the prudent man replies,
'Against Ulysses shall thy anger rise?
Loved and adored, O goddess, as thou art,   275
Forgive the weakness of a human heart.
Though well I see thy graces far above
The dear, though mortal, object of my love,
Of youth eternal well the difference know,
And the short date of fading charms below;   280
Yet every day, while absent thus I roam,

I languish to return, and die at home.
Whate'er the gods shall destine me to bear
In the black ocean, or the watery war,
'Tis mine to master with a constant mind,   285
Inured to perils, to the worst resigned.
By seas, by wars, so many dangers run,
Still I can suffer; their high will be done!'

Ulysses sets off, but as he approaches Phaeacia, Neptune stirs up a
storm, and he is swept overboard. He swims for two days, and is
eventually washed up on the rocky coast of Phaeacia. He sleeps
beneath the shade of two olive trees.

from **Book 6**

Nausicaa, daughter of Alcinoüs, King of Phaeacia, is commanded by
Minerva in a dream to go to the stream by the sea-shore and wash her
wedding robes. She sets out with her maidens.

Now mounting the gay seat, the silken reins   95
Shine in her hand; along the sounding plains
Swift fly the mules; nor rode the nymph alone.
Around, a bevy of bright damsels shone.
They seek the cisterns where Phaeacian dames
Wash their fair garments in the limpid streams,   100
Where, gathering into depth from falling rills,
The lucid wave a spacious basin fills.
The mules unharnessed range beside the main,
Or crop the verdant herbage of the plain.
Then emulous the royal robes they lave,   105
And plunge the vestures in the cleansing wave;
The vestures, cleansed, o'erspread the shelly sand,
Their snowy lustre whitens all the strand.
Then with a short repast relieve their toil,
And o'er their limbs diffuse ambrosial oil;   110

And, while the robes imbibe the solar ray,
O'er the green mead the sporting virgins play,
Their shining veils unbound. Along the skies
Tossed, and retossed, the ball incessant flies.
They sport, they feast, Nausicaa lifts her voice,   115
And warbling sweet, makes earth and heaven rejoice.
        As when o'er Erymanth Diana roves,
Or wide Täygetus' resounding groves;
A sylvan train the huntress queen surrounds,
Her rattling quiver from her shoulder sounds;   120
Fierce in the sport, along the mountain brow
They bay the boar, or chase the bounding roe;
High o'er the lawn, with more majestic pace,
Above the nymphs she treads with stately grace;
Distinguished excellence the goddess proves;   125
Exults Latona, as the virgin moves:
With equal grace Nausicaa trod the plain,
And shone transcendent o'er the beauteous train.
        Meantime (the care and favourite of the skies),
Wrapped in embowering shade, Ulysses lies,   130
His woes forgot. But Pallas now addressed
To break the bands of all-composing rest.
Forth from her snowy hand Nausicaa threw
The various ball; the ball erroneous flew,
And swam the stream; loud shrieks the virgin train,   135
And the loud shriek redoubles from the main.
Waked by the shrilling sound, Ulysses rose,
And to the deaf woods wailing, breathed his woes:
        'Ah me! on what inhospitable coast,
On what new region is Ulysses tossed?   140
Possessed by wild barbarians fierce in arms,
Or men, whose bosom tender pity warms?
What sounds are these that gather from the shores?
The voice of nymphs that haunt the sylvan bowers,
The fair-haired dryads of the shady wood,   145
Or azure daughters of the silver flood?
Or human voice? But issuing from the shades
Why cease I straight to learn what sound invades?'
        Then, where the grove with leaves umbrageous bends,
With forceful strength a branch the hero rends;   150

Around his loins the verdant cincture spreads
A wreathy foliage, and concealing shades.
As when a lion in the midnight hours
Beat by rude blasts, and wet with wintery showers,
Descends terrific from the mountain's brow, 155
With living flames his rolling eyeballs glow;
With conscious strength elate, he bends his way,
Majestically fierce, to seize his prey
The steer or stag; or with keen hunger bold
Springs o'er the fence, and dissipates the fold. 160
No less a terror, from the neighbouring groves,
Rough from the tossing surge, Ulysses moves;
Urged on by want, and recent from the storms;
The brackish ooze his manly grace deforms.
Wide o'er the shore with many a piercing cry 165
To rocks, to caves, the frighted virgins fly;
All but the nymph; the nymph stood fixed alone,
By Pallas armed with boldness not her own.
Meantime in dubious thought the king awaits,
And self-considering, as he stands, debates, 170
Distant his mournful story to declare,
Or prostrate at her knee address the prayer.
But, fearful to offend, by wisdom swayed,
At awful distance he accosts the maid:
　　　'If from the skies a goddess, or if earth, 175
Imperial virgin, boast thy glorious birth,
To thee I bend! If in that bright disguise
Thou visit earth, a daughter of the skies,
Hail, Dian, hail! The huntress of the groves
So shines majestic, and so stately moves, 180
So breathes an air divine! But if thy race
Be mortal, and this earth thy native place,
Blessed is the father from whose loins you sprung,
Blessed is the mother at whose breast you hung,
Blessed are the brethren who thy blood divide, 185
To such a miracle of charms allied;
Joyful they see applauding princes gaze,
When stately in the dance you swim th' harmonious maze.
But blessed o'er all the youth with heavenly charms,
Who clasps the bright perfection in his arms! 190

Never, I never viewed till this blessed hour
Such finished grace! I gaze and I adore!
Thus seems the palm with stately honours crowned
By Phoebus' altars; thus o'erlooks the ground
The pride of Delos. (By the Delian coast   195
I voyaged, leader of a warrior host,
But ah, how changed! From thence my sorrow flows;
O fatal voyage, source of all my woes!).
Raptured I stood, and, as this hour amazed,
With reverence at the lofty wonder gazed.   200
Raptured I stand; for earth ne'er knew to bear
A plant so stately, or a nymph so fair.
Awed from access, I lift my suppliant hands,
For Misery, O queen, before thee stands!
Twice ten tempestuous nights I rolled, resigned   205
To roaring billows and the warring wind;
Heaven bade the deep to spare, but heaven my foe
Spares only to inflict some mightier woe!
Inured to cares, to death in all its forms,
Outcast I rove, familiar with the storms!   210
Once more I view the face of humankind;
Oh let soft pity touch thy generous mind!
Unconscious of what air I breathe, I stand
Naked, defenceless on a foreign land.
Propitious to my wants, a vest supply   215
To guard the wretched from th' inclement sky:
So may the gods who heaven and earth control,
Crown the chaste wishes of thy virtuous soul,
On thy soft hours their choicest blessings shed;
Blessed with a husband be thy bridal bed,   220
Blessed be thy husband with a blooming race,
And lasting union crown your blissful days!
The gods, when they supremely bless, bestow
Firm union on their favourites below;
Then Envy grieves, with inly-pining Hate;   225
The good exult, and heaven is in our state.'

*Nausicaa bids her maidens feed and wash the stranger, then tells him
to follow her, after a discreet interval, to her father's court.*

from **Book 7**

Ulysses is conducted by Minerva to Alcinoüs' palace. Near the gates is Alcinoüs' garden.

Close to the gates a spacious garden lies,
From storms defended, and inclement skies.
Four acres was th' allotted space of ground,
Fenced with a green enclosure all around.   145
Tall thriving trees confessed the fruitful mould;
The reddening apple ripens here to gold,
Here the blue fig with luscious juice o'erflows,
With deeper red the full pomegranate glows,
The branch here bends beneath the weighty pear,   150
And verdant olives flourish round the year.
The balmy spirit of the western gale
Eternal breathes on fruits untaught to fail:
Each dropping pear a following pear supplies,
On apples apples, figs on figs arise.   155
The same mild season gives the blooms to blow,
The buds to harden, and the fruits to grow.
Here ordered vines in equal ranks appear,
With all th' united labours of the year;
Some t' unload the fertile branches run,   160
Some dry the blackening clusters in the sun,
Others to tread the liquid harvest join,
The groaning presses foam with floods of wine.
Here are the vines in early flower descried,
Here grapes discoloured on the sunny side,   165
And there in autumn's richest purple dyed.
Beds of all various herbs, for ever green,
In beauteous order terminate the scene.
Two plenteous fountains the whole prospect crowned;
This through the gardens leads its streams around,   170
Visits each plant, and waters all the ground,
While that in pipes beneath the palace flows,
And thence its current on the town bestows;
To various use their various streams they bring,
The people one, and one supplies the king.   175

Ulysses is hospitably received by King Alcinoüs and Queen Aretè. He tells them of his journey from Calypso's isle. Alcinoüs thinks Ulysses a suitable son-in-law, but will not detain him against his wishes.

from **Book 8**

After games, Ulysses is presented with fine gifts, and a bath is prepared for his refreshment.

He bathes; the damsels with officious toil,
Shed sweets, shed unguents, in a shower of oil,
Then o'er his limbs a gorgeous robe he spreads,
And to the feast magnificently treads.
Full where the dome its shining valves expands,   495
Nausicaa blooming as a goddess stands;
With wondering eyes the hero she surveyed,
And graceful thus began the royal maid:
     'Hail god-like stranger! and when heaven restores
To thy fond wish thy long-expected shores,   500
This ever grateful in remembrance bear,
To me thou ow'st, to me, the vital air.'
     'O royal maid,' Ulysses straight returns,
'Whose worth the splendours of thy race adorns,
So may dread Jove, whose arm in vengeance forms   505
The writhen bolt, and blackens heaven with storms,
Restore me safe, through weary wanderings tossed,
To my dear country's ever-pleasing coast,
As while the spirit in this bosom glows,
To thee, my goddess, I address my vows: 510
My life, thy gift I boast!' He said, and sat
Fast by Alcinoüs on a throne of state.

from **Book 9**

They feast, and Ulysses narrates his adventures after the fall of Troy.
Having encountered the Cicones and Lotophagi, the Ithacans arrived at
the land of Cyclopes, and discovered Polyphemus' cave. Ulysses,
curious to see the monster, awaited his return. Eventually he arrived.

'Near half a forest on his back he bore,
And cast the ponderous burden at the door.
It thundered as it fell. We trembled then,
And sought the deep recesses of the den.
Now driv'n before him, through the arching rock,   280
Came tumbling, heaps on heaps, th' unnumbered flock:
Big-uddered ewes, and goats of female kind
(The males were penned in outward courts behind).
Then, heaved on high, a rock's enormous weight
To the cave's mouth he rolled, and closed the gate   285
(Scarce twenty four-wheeled cars, compact and strong,
The massy load could bear, or roll along).
He next betakes him to his evening cares,
And sitting down, to milk his flocks prepares;
Of half their udders eases first the dams,   290
Then to the mother's teat submits the lambs.
Half the white stream to hardening cheese he pressed,
And high in wicker baskets heaped, the rest
Reserved in bowls, supplied his nightly feast.
His labour done, he fired the pile that gave   295
A sudden blaze, and lighted all the cave.
We stand discovered by the rising fires;
Askance the giant glares, and thus enquires:
    "What are ye, guests? On what adventure, say,
Thus far ye wander through the watery way?   300
Pirates perhaps, who seek through seas unknown
The lives of others, and expose your own?"
    His voice like thunder through the cavern sounds;
My bold companions thrilling fear confounds,
Appalled at sight of more than mortal man!   305
At length, with heart recovered, I began:
    "From Troy's famed fields, sad wanderers o'er the
                                                          main,

Behold the relics of the Grecian train!
Through various seas by various perils tossed,
And forced by storms, unwilling, on your coast,   310
Far from our destined course, and native land,
Such was our fate, and such high Jove's command!
Nor what we are befits us to disclaim,
Atrides' friends (in arms a mighty name),
Who taught proud Troy and all her sons to bow;   315
Victors of late, but humble suppliants now!
Low at thy knee thy succour we implore;
Respect us, human, and relieve us, poor.
At least some hospitable gift bestow;
'Tis what the happy to th' unhappy owe,   320
'Tis what the gods require – those gods revere;
The poor and stranger are their constant care;
To Jove their cause, and their revenge belongs,
He wanders with them, and he feels their wrongs."
     "Fools that ye are!" the savage thus replies,   325
His inward fury blazing at his eyes,
"Or strangers, distant far from our abodes,
To bid me reverence or regard the gods.
Know then we Cyclopes are a race above
Those air-bred people, and their goat-nursed Jove: 330
And learn, our power proceeds with thee and thine,
Not as he wills, but as ourselves incline.
But answer, the good ship that brought ye o'er,
Where lies she anchored? Near, or off the shore?"
     Thus he. His meditated fraud I find,   335
(Versed in the turns of various humankind)
And cautious, thus: "Against a dreadful rock,
Fast by your shore the gallant vessel broke;
Scarce with these few I scaped, of all my train,
Whom angry Neptune whelmed beneath the main;   340
The scattered wreck the winds blew back again."
     He answered with his deed. His bloody hand
Snatched two, unhappy, of my martial band;
And dashed like dogs against the stony floor:
The pavement swims with brains and mingled gore.   345
Torn limb from limb, he spreads his horrid feast,
And fierce devours it like a mountain beast:

He sucks the marrow, and the blood he drains,
Nor entrails, flesh, nor solid bone remains.
We see the death from which we cannot move,   350
And, humbled, groan beneath the hand of Jove.
His ample maw with human carnage filled,
A milky deluge next the giant swilled;
Then stretched in length o'er half the caverned rock,
Lay senseless and supine amidst the flock.   355
To seize the time, and with a sudden wound
To fix the slumbering monster to the ground,
My soul impels me, and in act I stand
To draw the sword, but wisdom held my hand.
A deed so rash had finished all our fate;   360
No mortal forces from the lofty gate
Could roll the rock. In hopeless grief we lay,
And sigh, expecting the return of day.'

The next day, Polyphemus devoured another two of Ulysses' men.
While the giant was away tending his flocks, Ulysses meditated his
plan of escape. The Ithacans sharpened the end of Polyphemus' club.
On the giant's return, Ulysses plied him with wine, telling him that he
was called 'Noman'. Polyphemus pledged that 'Noman' would be the
last of the visitors to be devoured, then fell into a deep sleep. Ulysses
now put his plan into action.

'Sudden I stir the embers, and inspire   445
With animating breath the seeds of fire;
Each drooping spirit with bold words repair,
And urge my train the dreadful deed to dare.
The stake now glowed beneath the burning bed,
Green as it was, and sparkled fiery red.   450
Then forth the vengeful instrument I bring;
With beating hearts my fellows form a ring.
Urged by some present god, they swift let fall
The pointed torment on his visual ball.
Myself above them from a rising ground   455
Guide the sharp stake, and twirl it round and round;
As when a shipwright stands his workmen o'er,
Who plie the wimble, some huge beam to bore;

Urged on all hands it nimbly spins about,
The grain deep-piercing till it scoops it out: 460
In his broad eye so whirls the fiery wood,
From the pierced pupil spouts the boiling blood;
Singed are his brows; the scorching lids grow black;
The jelly bubbles, and the fibres crack.
And as when armourers temper in the ford   465
The keen-edged pole-axe, or the shining sword,
The red-hot metal hisses in the lake,
Thus in his eyeball hissed the plunging stake.
He sends a dreadful groan; the rocks around
Through all their inmost winding caves resound.   470
Scared we receded. Forth, with frantic hand
He tore, and dashed on earth the gory brand;
Then calls the Cyclopes, all that round him dwell,
With voice like thunder, and a direful yell.
From all their dens the one-eyed race repair,   475
From rifted rocks, and mountains bleak in air.
All haste, assembled at his well-known roar,
Enquire the cause, and crowd the cavern door.
          "What hurts thee, Polypheme? What strange affright
Thus breaks our slumbers, and disturbs the night?   480
Does any mortal in th' unguarded hour
Of sleep, oppress thee, or by fraud or power?
Or thieves insidious thy fair flock surprize?"
          Thus they; the Cyclop from his den replies:
"Friends, Noman kills me; Noman in the hour   485
Of sleep oppresses me with fraudful power."
"If no man hurt thee, but the hand divine
Inflict disease, it fits thee to resign:
To Jove or to thy father Neptune pray,"
The brethren cried, and instant strode away.   490
          Joy touched my secret soul, and conscious heart,
Pleased with th' effect of conduct and of art.
Meantime the Cyclop, raging with his wound,
Spreads his wide arms, and searches round and round;
At last, the stone removing from the gate,   495
With hands extended in the midst he sat;
And searched each passing sheep, and felt it o'er,
Secure to seize us ere we reached the door

(Such as his shallow wit, he deemed was mine).
But secret I revolved the deep design;   500
'Twas for our lives my labouring bosom wrought,
Each scheme I turned, and sharpened every thought;
This way and that, I cast to save my friends,
Till one resolve my varying counsel ends.

      Strong were the rams, with native purple fair,   505
Well fed, and largest of the fleecy care.
These three and three, with osier bands we tied
(The twining bands the Cyclop's bed supplied),
The midmost bore a man; the outward two
Secured each side; so bound we all the crew.   510
One ram remained, the leader of the flock;
In his deep fleece my grasping hands I lock,
And fast beneath, in woolly curls inwove,
There cling implicit, and confide in Jove.
When rosy morning glimmered o'er the dales,   515
He drove to pasture all the lusty males;
The ewes still folded, with distended thighs
Unmilked, lay bleating in distressful cries.
But heedless of those cares, with anguish stung,
He felt their fleeces as they passed along –   520
Fool that he was! – and let them safely go,
All unsuspecting of their freight below.

      The master ram at last approached the gate,
Charged with his wool, and with Ulysses' fate.
Him while he passed the monster blind bespoke: 525
"What makes my ram the lag of all the flock?
First thou wert wont to crop the flowery mead,
First to the field and river's bank to lead,
And first with stately step at evening hour
Thy fleecy fellows usher to their bower.   530
Now far the last, with pensive pace and slow
Thou mov'st, as conscious of thy master's woe!
Seest thou these lids that now unfold in vain,
The deed of Noman and his wicked train?
Oh, didst thou feel for thy afflicted lord,   535
And would but fate the power of speech afford;
Soon might'st thou tell me where in secret here

The dastard lurks, all trembling with his fear.
Swung round and round, and dashed from rock to rock,
His battered brains should on the pavement smoke.   540
No ease, no pleasure my sad heart receives,
While such a monster as vile Noman lives!"
          The giant spoke, and through the hollow rock
Dismissed the ram, the father of the flock.
No sooner freed, and through th' enclosure passed,   545
First I release my self, my fellows last:
Fat sheep and goats in throngs we drive before,
And reach our vessel on the winding shore.'

*As the Ithacans sailed away, Ulysses could not resist taunting the
Cyclops and revealing his true identity. Polyphemus had been told that
he was fated to be blinded by someone called 'Ulysses', but had
expected an heroic adversary, not a cunning deceiver. In his rage, the
Cyclops prayed to his father Neptune:*

' "Hear me, O Neptune, thou whose arms are hurled
From shore to shore, and gird the solid world!
If thine I am, nor thou my birth disown,
And if th' unhappy Cyclop be thy son,   620
Let not Ulysses breathe his native air,
Laertes' son, of Ithaca the fair.
If to review his country be his fate,
Be it through toils and sufferings, long and late;
His lost companions let him first deplore;   625
Some vessel, not his own, transport him o'er;
And when at home from foreign sufferings freed,
More near and deep, domestic woes succeed!"
          With imprecations thus he filled the air,
And angry Neptune heard th' unrighteous prayer.'   630

from **Book 10**

Ulysses narrates how he then visited the island of Aeolus and the land
of the Laestrygonians, where he lost eleven of his ships. With his one
remaining vessel, he arrived at the island of the sorceress, Circe.
Mindful of possible danger, Ulysses divided his men into two parties.
One of them, led by Eurylochus, discovered Circe's palace.

'The palace in a woody vale they found,   240
High raised of stone, a shaded space around,
Where mountain wolves and brindled lions roam
By magic tamed, familiar to the dome.
With gentle blandishment our men they meet,
And wag their tails, and fawning lick their feet.   245
As from some feast a man returning late,
His faithful dogs all meet him at the gate,
Rejoicing round, some morsel to receive
(Such as the good man ever used to give),
Domestic thus the grisly beasts drew near;   250
They gaze with wonder, not unmixed with fear.
Now on the threshold of the dome they stood,
And heard a voice resounding through the wood.
Placed at her loom within, the goddess sung;
The vaulted roofs and solid pavement rung.   255
O'er the fair web the rising figures shine,
Immortal labour, worthy hands divine!
Polites to the rest the question moved
(A gallant leader, and a man I loved):
    "What voice celestial, chanting to the loom   260
Or nymph, or goddess, echoes from the room?
Say shall we seek access?" With that they call,
And wide unfold the portals of the hall.
    The goddess rising, asks her guests to stay,
Who blindly follow where she leads the way.   265
Eurylochus alone of all the band,
Suspecting fraud, more prudently remained.
On thrones around, with downy coverings graced,
With semblance fair th' unhappy men she placed.
Milk newly pressed, the sacred flower of wheat,   270

And honey fresh, and Pramnian wines the treat;
But venomed was the bread, and mixed the bowl,
With drugs of force to darken all the soul.
Soon in the luscious feast themselves they lost,
And drank oblivion of their native coast.   275
Instant her circling wand the goddess waves,
To hogs transforms 'em, and the sty receives.
No more was seen the human form divine,
Head, face and members bristle into swine,
Still cursed with sense, their minds remains alone,   280
And their own voice affrights them when they groan.
Meanwhile the goddess in disdain bestows
The mast and acorn – brutal food! – and strows
The fruits of cornel, as their feast, around,
Now prone, and grovelling on unsavoury ground.'   285

*Warned by Eurylochus of the danger, and armed by Hermes with an
antidote against Circe's charms, Ulysses made his way to Circe's
palace.*

'Arrived, before the lofty gates I stayed,
The lofty gates the goddess wide displayed;
She leads before, and to the feast invites;
I follow sadly to the magic rites.
Radiant with starry studs, a silver seat   375
Received my limbs; a footstool eased my feet.
She mixed the potion, fraudulent of soul;
The poison mantled in the golden bowl.
I took, and quaffed it, confident in heaven,
Then waved the wand, and then the word was given.   380
"Hence, to thy fellows!" dreadful she began,
"Go, be a beast!" I heard – and yet was man.
          Then sudden whirling like a waving flame
My beamy falchion, I assault the dame.
Struck with unusual fear, she trembling cries,   385
She faints, she falls, she lifts her weeping eyes.
          "What art thou? Say, from whence, from whom you
                                                    came?
O more than human! Tell thy race, thy name.
Amazing strength, these poisons to sustain!

Not mortal thou, nor mortal is thy brain.   390
Or art thou he: the man to come (foretold
By Hermes powerful with the wand of gold),
The man from Troy, who wandered ocean round,
The man, for wisdom's various arts renowned,
Ulysses? Oh, thy threatening fury cease;   395
Sheathe thy bright sword, and join our hands in peace;
Let mutual joys our mutual trust combine,
And love and love-born confidence be thine."
    "And how, dread Circe," furious I rejoin,
"Can love and love-born confidence be mine,   400
Beneath thy charms when my companions groan,
Transformed to beasts, with accents not their own?
O thou of fraudful heart, shall I be led
To share thy feast-rites, or ascend thy bed;
That, all unarmed, thy vengeance may have vent,   405
And magic bind me, cold and impotent?
Celestial as thou art, yet stand denied;
Or swear that oath by which the gods are tied,
Swear in thy soul no latent frauds remain,
Swear, by the vow which never can be vain."   410
    The goddess swore, then seized my hand, and led
To the sweet transports of the genial bed.
Ministrant to their queen, with busy care
Four faithful handmaids the soft rites prepare;
Nymphs sprung from fountains, or from shady woods,   415
Or the fair offspring of the sacred floods.
One o'er the couches painted carpets threw,
Whose purple lustre glowed against the view:
White linen lay beneath. Another placed
The silver stands with golden flaskets graced;   420
With dulcet beverage this the beaker crowned,
Fair in the midst, with gilded cups around,
That in the tripod o'er the kindled pile
The water pours; the bubbling waters boil.
An ample vase receives the smoking wave,   425
And in the bath prepared my limbs I lave;
Reviving sweets repair the mind's decay,
And take the painful sense of toil away.

A vest and tunic o'er me next she threw,
Fresh from the bath and dropping balmy dew;　　　430
Then led and placed me on the sovereign seat,
With carpets spread; a footstool at my feet.
The golden ewer a nymph obsequious brings,
Replenished from the cool, translucent springs;
With copious water the bright vase supplies　　　435
A silver laver of capacious size.
I washed. The table in fair order spread,
They heap the glittering canisters with bread;
Viands of various kinds allure the taste,
Of choicest sort and savour, rich repast!　　　440
Circe in vain invites the feast to share;
Absent I ponder, and absorbed in care,
While scenes of woe rose anxious in my breast,
The queen beheld me, and these words addressed:
　　　"Why sits Ulysses silent and apart?　　　445
Some hoard of grief close-harboured at his heart.
Untouched before thee stand the cates divine,
And unregarded laughs the rosy wine.
Can yet a doubt, or any dread remain,
When sworn that oath which never can be vain?"　　　450
　　　I answered: "Goddess, human is thy breast,
By justice swayed, by tender pity pressed;
Ill fits it me, whose friends are sunk to beasts,
To quaff thy bowls, or riot in thy feasts.
Me wouldst thou please? For them thy cares employ,　　　455
And them to me restore, and me to joy."
　　　With that, she parted; in her potent hand
She bore the virtue of the magic wand.
Then hastening to the styes, set wide the door,
Urged forth, and drove the bristly herd before;　　　460
Unwieldy, out they rushed, with general cry,
Enormous beasts dishonest to the eye.
Now touched by counter-charms, they change again,
And stand majestic, and recalled to men.
Those hairs of late that bristled every part,　　　465
Fall off, miraculous effect of art!
Till all the form in full proportion rise,

More young, more large, more graceful to my eyes.
They saw, they knew me, and with eager pace
Clung to their master in a long embrace: 470
Sad, pleasing sight! With tears each eye ran o'er,
And sobs of joy re-echoed through the bower:
Ev'n Circe wept, her adamantine heart
Felt pity enter, and sustained her part.'

from **Book 11**

Ulysses and his men stayed with Circe for a year. Then, on Circe's advice, Ulysses visited the land of the Cimmerians, where Tiresias warned him of the dangers still facing him. He met the shade of his mother, Anticlea, and asked her for news of Laertes, Telemachus, and Penelope.

'Thus I, and thus the parent shade returns:
"Thee, ever thee, thy faithful consort mourns;
Whether the night descends, or day prevails,   220
Thee she by night, and thee by day bewails.
Thee in Telemachus thy realm obeys;
In sacred groves celestial rites he pays,
And shares the banquet in superior state,
Graced with such honours as become the great.   225
Thy sire in solitude foments his care:
The court is joyless, for thou art not there!
No costly carpets raise his hoary head,
No rich embroidery shines to grace his bed;
Ev'n when keen winter freezes in the skies,   230
Ranked with his slaves, on earth the monarch lies;
Deep are his sighs, his visage pale, his dress
The garb of woe and habit of distress.
And when the autumn takes his annual round,
The leafy honours scattering on the ground;   235
Regardless of his years, abroad he lies,
His bed the leaves, his canopy the skies.

Thus cares on cares his painful days consume,
And bow his age with sorrow to the tomb!
    For thee, my son, I wept my life away,   240
For thee through hell's eternal dungeons stray;
Nor came my fate by lingering pains and slow,
Nor bent the silver-shafted queen her bow;
No dire disease bereaved me of my breath –
Thou, thou, my son wert my disease and death;   245
Unkindly with my love my son conspired,
For thee I lived, for absent thee expired." '

Later, Ulysses encountered the shade of Achilles.

    'Through the thick gloom his friend Achilles knew,
And as he speaks the tears descend in dew:
"Com'st thou alive to view the Stygian bounds,
Where the wan spectres walk eternal rounds;
Nor fear'st the dark and dismal waste to tread,   585
Thronged with pale ghosts, familiar with the dead?"
    To whom with sighs: "I pass these dreadful gates
To seek the Theban, and consult the Fates:
For still distressed I rove from coast to coast,
Lost to my friends, and to my country lost.   590
But sure the eye of time beholds no name
So blessed as thine in all the rolls of fame;
Alive, we hailed thee with our guardian gods,
And, dead, thou rul'st a king in these abodes."
    "Talk not of ruling in this dolorous gloom,   595
Nor think vain words," he cried, "can ease my doom;
Rather I choose laboriously to bear
A weight of woes, and breathe the vital air,
A slave to some poor hind that toils for bread,
Than reign the sceptred monarch of the dead!" '   600

from **Book 12**

After leaving Circe's island, Ulysses encountered the Sirens, the first of the dangers of which the sorceress had forewarned him.

'While yet I speak the wingèd galley flies,   200
And lo! the Siren shores like mists arise.
Sunk were at once the winds, the air above,
And waves below, at once forgot to move!
Some demon calmed the air, and smoothed the deep,
Hushed the loud winds, and charmed the waves to sleep.   205
Now every sail we furl, each oar we ply;
Lashed by the stroke the frothy waters fly.
The ductile wax with busy hands I mould,
And cleft in fragments, and the fragments rolled;
Th' aërial region now grew warm with day,   210
The wax dissolved beneath the burning ray;
Then every ear I barred against the strain,
And from access of frenzy locked the brain.
Now round the mast my mates the fetters rolled,
And bound me limb by limb, with fold on fold.   215
Then bending to the stroke, the active train
Plunge all at once their oars, and cleave the main.
        While to the shore the rapid vessel flies,
Our swift approach the Siren choir descries;
Celestial music warbles from their tongue,   220
And thus the sweet deluders tune the song:
"O stay, O pride of Greece! Ulysses stay!
O cease thy course, and listen to our lay!
Blessed is the man ordained our voice to hear,
The song instructs the soul, and charms the ear.   225
Approach! Thy soul shall into raptures rise!
Approach, and learn new wisdom from the wise!
We know whate'er the kings of mighty name
Achieved at Ilion in the field of fame;
Whate'er beneath the sun's bright journey lies.   230
O stay, and learn new wisdom from the wise!"
        Thus the sweet charmers warbled o'er the main;
My soul takes wing to meet the heavenly strain;

I give the sign, and struggle to be free:
Swift row my mates, and shoot along the sea;   235
New chains they add, and rapid urge the way,
Till dying off, the distant sounds decay:
Then, scudding swiftly from the dangerous ground,
The deafened ear unlocked, the chains unbound.'

*The Ithacans escaped Scylla and Charybdis, but Ulysses' men were all
lost when, going against Ulysses' orders, they slaughtered the Oxen of
the Sun. Ulysses alone escaped, and eventually reached Calypso's isle.*

from **Book 13**

*Having completed the narration of his adventures, Ulysses is
transported by the Phaeacians to Ithaca, with treasure given him by
Alcinoüs.*

Thus with spread sails the wingèd galley flies;
Less swift an eagle cuts the liquid skies: 105
Divine Ulysses was her sacred load,
A man in wisdom equal to a god!
Much danger long and mighty toils he bore,
In storms by sea, and combats on the shore;
All which soft sleep now banished from his breast,   110
Wrapped in a pleasing, deep, and death-like rest.
But when the morning star with early ray
Flamed in the front of heaven, and promised day;
Like distant clouds the mariner descries
Fair Ithaca's emerging hills arise.   115
Far from the town a spacious port appears,
Sacred to Phorcys' power, whose name it bears.
Two craggy rocks projecting to the main
The roaring wind's tempestuous rage restrain;
Within, the waves in softer murmurs glide,   120

And ships secure without their hawsers ride.
High at the head a branching olive grows,
And crowns the pointed cliffs with shady boughs.
Beneath, a gloomy grotto's cool recess
Delights the Nereids of the neighbouring seas,   125
Where bowls and urns were formed of living stone,
And massy beams in native marble shone;
On which the labours of the nymphs were rolled,
Their webs divine of purple mixed with gold.
Within the cave, the clustering bees attend   130
Their waxen works, or from the roof depend.
Perpetual waters o'er the pavement glide,
Two marble doors unfold on either side;
Sacred the south, by which the gods descend,
But mortals enter at the northern end.   135
     Thither they bent, and hauled their ship to land;
The crooked keel divides the yellow sand.
Ulysses sleeping on his couch they bore,
And gently placed him on the rocky shore.
His treasures next, Alcinoüs' gifts, they laid   140
In the wild olive's unfrequented shade,
Secure from theft; then launched the bark again,
Resumed their oars, and measured back the main.

When Ulysses awakes, Minerva, who has shrouded the region in an
obscuring cloud, visits him in the form of a young shepherd. Wary of
revealing his true identity, Ulysses pretends to be a Cretan exile.
Minerva then reveals herself to him.

     Thus while he spoke, the blue-eyed maid began
With pleasing smiles to view the godlike man,
Then changed her form; and now, divinely bright,
Jove's heavenly daughter stood confessed to sight.   330
Like a fair virgin in her beauty's bloom,
Skilled in th' illustrious labours of the loom.
     'O still the same Ulysses!' she rejoined,
'In useful craft successfully refined!
Artful in speech, in action, and in mind!   335
Sufficed it not that, thy long labours passed,

Secure thou seest thy native shore at last?
But this to me, who, like thyself, excel
In arts of counsel, and dissembling well!
To me, whose wit exceeds the powers divine,   340
No less than mortals are surpassed by thine!'

With Minerva's help, and disguised as a beggar, he makes his way to
the hut of the faithful old swineherd, Eumaeus.

from Book 14

Eumaeus at his sylvan lodge he sought,   5
A faithful servant, and without a fault.
Ulysses found him, busied as he sat
Before the threshold of his rustic gate;
Around the mansion in a circle shone
A rural portico of rugged stone   10
(In absence of his lord, with honest toil,
His own industrious hands had raised the pile);
The wall was stone from neighbouring quarries borne,
Encircled with a fence of native thorn,
And strong with pales, by many a weary stroke   15
Of stubborn labour hewn from heart of oak,
Frequent and thick. Within the space were reared
Twelve ample cells, the lodgements of his herd.
Full fifty pregnant females each contained,
The males without (a smaller race) remained,   20
Doomed to supply the suitors' wasteful feast,
A stock by daily luxury decreased;
Now scarce four hundred left. These to defend,
Four savage dogs, a watchful guard, attend.
Here sat Eumaeus, and his cares applied   25
To form strong buskins of well-seasoned hide.
Of four assistants who his labour share,
Three now were absent on the rural care;

The fourth drove victims to the suitor-train:
But he, of ancient faith, a simple swain,   30
Sighed, while he furnished the luxurious board,
And wearied heaven with wishes for his lord.

Eumaeus receives Ulysses hospitably.

His vest succinct then girding round his waist,
Forth rushed the swain with hospitable haste,
Straight to the lodgements of his herd he run,   85
Where the fat porkers slept beneath the sun;
Of two, his cutlass launched the spouting blood;
These quartered, singed, and fixed on forks of wood,
All hasty on the hissing coals he threw;
And smoking back the tasteful viands drew,   90
Broachers and all; then on the board displayed
The ready meal before Ulysses laid,
With flour imbrowned; next mingled wine yet new,
And luscious as the bee's nectareous dew;
Then sat companion of the friendly feast,   95
With open look, and thus bespoke his guest:
        'Take with free welcome what our hands prepare,
Such food as falls to simple servants' share;
The best our lords consume; those thoughtless peers,
Rich without bounty, guilty without fears!   100
Yet sure the gods their impious acts detest,
And honour justice and the righteous breast.'

*Meanwhile Minerva helps Telemachus to avoid the ambush which the
suitors have prepared for him on his return, and tells him to spend his
first night on Ithaca at Eumaeus' hut.*

from **Book 16**

Father and son meet, and Minerva removes Ulysses' disguise, giving him a majestic aura. At first Telemachus thinks himself in the presence of a god.

Then with surprise – surprise chastised by fears –
'How art thou changed!' he cried, 'A god appears!
Far other vests thy limbs majestic grace,
Far other glories lighten from thy face!
If heaven be thy abode, with pious care   200
Lo, I the ready sacrifice prepare!
Lo, gifts of laboured gold adorn thy shrine,
To win thy grace: O save us, power divine!'
       'Few are my days,' Ulysses made reply,
'Nor I, alas, descendant of the sky!   205
I am thy father – O my son, my son!
That father, for whose sake thy days have run
One scene of woe, to endless cares consigned,
And outraged by the wrongs of base mankind.'
       Then rushing to his arms, he kissed his boy   210
With the strong raptures of a parent's joy.
Tears bathe his cheek, and tears the ground bedew;
He strained him close, as to his breast he grew.
       'Ah me!' exclaims the prince with fond desire,
'Thou art not – no, thou can'st not be – my sire!   215
Heav'n such illusion only can impose,
By the false joy, to aggravate my woes.
Who but a god can change the general doom,
And give to withered age a youthful bloom?
Late, worn with years, in weeds obscene you trod,   220
Now clothed in majesty, you move a god!'
       'Forbear,' he cried, 'for heaven reserve that name;
Give to thy father but a father's claim;
Other Ulysses shalt thou never see:
I am Ulysses, I, my son, am he!   225
Twice ten sad years o'er earth and ocean tossed,
'Tis given at length to view my native coast.
Pallas, unconquered maid, my frame surrounds

With grace divine; her power admits no bounds.
She o'er my limbs old age and wrinkles shed;   230
Now strong as youth, magnificent I tread.
The gods with ease frail man depress, or raise,
Exalt the lowly, or the proud debase.'

      He spoke and sat. The prince with transport flew,
Hung round his neck, while tears his cheek bedew;   235
Nor less the father poured a social flood!
They wept abundant, and they wept aloud.
As the bold eagle with fierce sorrow stung,
Or parent vulture, mourns her ravished young –
They cry, they scream, their unfledged brood a prey   240
To some rude churl, and borne by stealth away –
So they aloud, and tears in tides had run,
Their grief unfinished with the setting sun.

from **Book 17**

*Ulysses and Eumaeus (to whom he has not yet revealed his identity)
go to the palace. Though Ulysses is disguised as a beggar, he is
recognized by his old dog, Argus.*

      Thus, near the gates conferring as they drew,
Argus, the dog, his ancient master knew;   345
He, not unconscious of the voice and tread,
Lifts to the sound his ear, and rears his head.
Bred by Ulysses, nourished at his board,
But ah, not fated long to please his lord!
To him, his swiftness and his strength were vain;   350
The voice of glory called him o'er the main.
Till then in every sylvan chase renowned,
With Argus, Argus, rung the woods around;
With him the youth pursued the goat or fawn,
Or traced the mazy leveret o'er the lawn.   355
Now left to man's ingratitude he lay,
Unhoused, neglected, in the public way,

And where on heaps the rich manure was spread,
Obscene with reptiles, took his sordid bed.
    He knew his lord; he knew, and strove to meet,   360
In vain he strove to crawl, and kiss his feet;
Yet – all he could – his tail, his ears, his eyes
Salute his master, and confess his joys.
Soft pity touched the mighty master's soul;
Adown his cheek a tear unbidden stole,   365
Stole unperceived; he turned his head, and dried
The drop humane, then thus impassioned cried:
    'What noble beast in this abandoned state
Lies here all helpless at Ulysses' gate?
His bulk and beauty speak no vulgar praise;   370
If, as he seems, he was in better days,
Some care his age deserves: or was he prized
For worthless beauty, therefore now despised?
Such dogs and men there are, mere things of state,
And always cherished by their friends, the great.'   375
    'Not Argus so,' Eumaeus thus rejoined,
'But served a master of a nobler kind,
Who never, never shall behold him more!
Long, long since perished on a distant shore!
Oh had you seen him, vigorous, bold and young,   380
Swift as a stag, and as a lion strong!
Him no fell savage on the plain withstood,
None 'scaped him, bosomed in the gloomy wood;
His eye how piercing, and his scent how true,
To wind the vapour in the tainted dew!   385
Such, when Ulysses left his natal coast;
Now years unnerve him, and his lord is lost!
The women keep the generous creature bare;
A sleek and idle race is all their care:
The master gone, the servants what restrains?   390
Or dwells humanity where riot reigns?
Jove fixed it certain, that whatever day
Makes man a slave, takes half his worth away.'
    This said, the honest herdsman strode before;
The musing monarch pauses at the door.   395
The dog, whom fate had granted to behold
His lord, when twenty tedious years had rolled,

Takes a last look, and, having seen him, dies;
So closed for ever faithful Argus' eyes!

from **Book 19**

*Penelope receives the disguised Ulysses hospitably. As Euryclea,
Ulysses' old nurse, is washing him, she recognizes an old boar-hunting
scar on his knee.*

Deep o'er his knee inseamed remained the scar,
Which noted token of the woodland war   545
When Euryclea found, th' ablution ceased;
Down dropped the leg, from her slack hand released;
The mingled fluids from the vase redound;
The vase reclining floats the floor around!
Smiles dewed with tears the pleasing strife expressed   550
Of grief, and joy, alternate in her breast.
Her fluttering words in melting murmurs died;
At length abrupt, 'My son! My king!' she cried.
His neck with fond embrace infolding fast,
Full on the queen her raptured eyes she cast,   555
Ardent to speak the monarch safe restored;
But studious to conceal her royal lord,
Minerva fixed her mind on views remote,
And from the present bliss abstracts her thought.
His hand to Euryclea's mouth applied,   560
        'Art thou foredoomed my pest?' the hero cried.
'Thy milky founts my infant lips have drained;
And have the Fates thy babbling age ordained
To violate the life thy youth sustained?
An exile have I told, with weeping eyes,   565
Full twenty annual suns in distant skies;
At length returned, some god inspires thy breast
To know thy king, and here I stand confessed.
This heaven-discovered truth to thee consigned,
Reserve, the treasure of thy inmost mind;   570

Else, if the gods my vengeful arm sustain,
And prostrate to my sword the suitor-train;
With their lewd mates, thy undistinguished age
Shall bleed, a victim to vindictive rage.'

    Then thus rejoined the dame, devoid of fear: 575
'What words, my son, have passed thy lips severe?
Deep in my soul the trust shall lodge secured,
With ribs of steel, and marble heart immured.
When heaven, auspicious to thy right avowed,
Shall prostrate to thy sword the suitor-crowd;   580
The deeds I'll blazon of the menial fair;
The lewd to death devote, the virtuous spare.'

from **Book 21**

To put an end to the suitors' harassment, Penelope agrees to marry the man who can string the bow of Ulysses, and shoot through twelve ringlets. Telemachus invites the suitors to try. Ulysses, having secretly arranged for the doors to be bolted, is allowed to take the bow, despite protests from Antinoüs.

    And now his well-known bow the master bore,
Turned on all sides, and viewed it o'er and o'er,
Lest time or worms had done the weapon wrong,
Its owner absent, and untried so long;   430
While some deriding: 'How he turns the bow!
Some other like it sure the man must know,
Or else would copy; or in bows he deals;
Perhaps he makes them, or perhaps he steals.'
'Heav'n to this wretch,' another cried, 'be kind!   435
And bless, in all to which he stands inclined,
With such good fortune as he now shall find.'
    Heedless he heard them; but disdained reply,
The bow perusing with exactest eye.
Then, as some heavenly minstrel, taught to sing   440
High notes, responsive to the trembling string,

To some new strain when he adapts the lyre,
Or the dumb lute refits with vocal wire,
Relaxes, strains, and draws them to and fro:
So the great master drew the mighty bow, 445
And drew with ease. One hand aloft displayed
The bending horns, and one the string essayed.
From his essaying hand the string let fly
Twanged short and sharp, like the shrill swallow's cry.
A general horror ran through all the race, 450
Sunk was each heart, and pale was every face.
Signs from above ensued: th' unfolding sky
In lightning burst; Jove thundered from on high.
Fired at the call of heaven's almighty lord,
He snatched the shaft that glittered on the board 455
(Fast by, the rest lay sleeping in the sheath,
But soon to fly, the messengers of death).
　　　Now sitting as he was, the cord he drew,
Through every ringlet levelling his view,
Then notched the shaft, released, and gave it wing; 460
The whizzing arrow vanished from the string,
Sung on direct, and threaded every ring.
The solid gate its fury scarcely bounds;
Pierced through and through, the solid gate resounds.

from **Book 22**

Ulysses kills Antinoüs, and reveals his own true identity.

When fierce the hero o'er the threshold strode;
Stripped of his rags, he blazed out like a god.
Full in their face the lifted bow he bore,
And quivered deaths, a formidable store;
Before his feet the rattling shower he threw, 5
And thus terrific, to the suitor crew:
'One venturous game this hand has won today,
Another, princes, yet remains to play;

Another mark our arrow must attain.
Phoebus assist, nor be the labour vain!'   10
      Swift as the word the parting arrow sings,
And bears thy fate, Antinoüs, on its wings:
Wretch that he was, of unprophetic soul!
High in his hands he reared the golden bowl;
Ev'n then to drain it lengthened out his breath,   15
Changed to the deep, the bitter draught of death:
For fate who feared amidst a feastful band?
And fate to numbers by a single hand?
Full through his throat Ulysses' weapon passed,
And pierced the neck. He falls, and breathes his last.   20
The tumbling goblet the wide floor o'erflows,
A stream of gore burst spouting from his nose;
Grim in convulsive agonies he sprawls:
Before him spurned, the loaded table falls,
And spreads the pavement with a mingled flood   25
Of floating meats, and wine, and human blood.
Amazed, confounded, as they saw him fall,
Uprose the throngs tumultuous round the hall;
O'er all the dome they cast a haggard eye,
Each looked for arms – in vain; no arms were nigh.   30
      'Aim'st thou at princes?' all amazed they said,
'Thy last of games unhappy hast thou played;
Thy erring shaft has made our bravest bleed,
And death, unlucky guest, attends thy deed.
Vultures shall tear thee' – thus incensed they spoke,   35
While each to chance ascribed the wondrous stroke;
Blind as they were; for death ev'n now invades
His destined prey, and wraps them all in shades.
Then grimly frowning with a dreadful look
That withered all their hearts, Ulysses spoke: 40
      'Dogs, ye have had your day! Ye feared no more
Ulysses vengeful from the Trojan shore,
While to your lust and spoil a guardless prey,
Our house, our wealth, our helpless handmaids lay.
Not so content, with bolder frenzy fired,   45
Ev'n to our bed presumptuous you aspired:
Laws or divine or human failed to move,
Or shame of men, or dread of gods above,

Heedless alike of infamy or praise,
Or fame's eternal voice in future days.   50
The hour of vengeance, wretches, now is come!
Impending fate is yours, and instant doom!'

*The suitors are slaughtered, one by one. Euryclea identifies the
handmaids who have been disloyal to Penelope. Ulysses orders that
they should be made to purify the room, and then be hanged.*

from **Book 23**

*Penelope is dumbfounded at the news of the suitors' death. But she is,
at first, wary of accepting their slayer as her long-lost husband. With
his heroic grace enhanced by Minerva, he provides her with
incontrovertible proof that he is, indeed, Ulysses.*

As by some artist to whom Vulcan gives
His heavenly skill, a breathing image lives;
By Pallas taught, he frames the wondrous mould,
And the pale silver glows with fusile gold: 160
So Pallas his heroic form improves
With bloom divine, and like a god he moves;
More high he treads, and issuing forth in state,
Radiant before his gazing consort sat.
    And, 'O my queen!' he cries, 'what power above   165
Has steeled that heart, averse to spousal love!
Canst thou, Penelope, when heaven restores
Thy lost Ulysses to his native shores,
Canst thou, oh cruel! unconcerned survey
Thy lost Ulysses, on this signal day?   170
Haste, Euryclea, and dispatchful spread
For me, and me alone, th' imperial bed:
My weary nature craves the balm of rest:
But heaven with adamant has armed her breast.'
    'Ah no!' she cries, 'a tender heart I bear,   175

A foe to pride; no adamant is there;
And now, ev'n now, it melts! For sure I see
Once more Ulysses my beloved in thee!
Fixed in my soul as when he sailed to Troy,
His image dwells: then haste the bed of joy!   180
Haste, from the bridal bower the bed translate,
Framed by his hand, and be it dressed in state!'
          Thus speaks the queen, still dubious, with disguise;
Touched at her words, the king with warmth replies:
'Alas for this! What mortal strength can move   185
Th' enormous burden, who but heaven above?
It mocks the weak attempts of human hands;
But the whole earth must move, if heaven commands.
Then hear sure evidence, while we display
Words sealed with sacred truth, and truth obey: 190
This hand the wonder framed; an olive spread
Full in the court its ever-verdant head.
Vast as some mighty column's bulk, on high
The huge trunk rose, and heaved into the sky;
Around the tree I raised a nuptial bower,   195
And roofed defensive of the storm and shower;
The spacious valve, with art inwrought, conjoins;
And the fair dome with polished marble shines.
I lopped the branchy head; aloft in twain
Severed the bole, and smoothed the shining grain;   200
Then posts, capacious of the frame, I raise,
And bore it, regular from space to space.
Athwart the frame, at equal distance lie
Thongs of tough hides, that boast a purple dye;
Then polishing the whole, the finished mould   205
With silver shone, with elephant, and gold.
But if o'erturned by rude, ungoverned hands,
Or still inviolate the olive stands,
'Tis thine, O queen, to say, and now impart,
If fears remain, or doubts distract thy heart?'   210
          While yet he speaks, her powers of life decay,
She sickens, trembles, falls, and faints away;
At length recovering, to his arms she flew,
And strained him close, as to his breast she grew;
The tears poured down amain, and, 'Oh,' she cries,   215

'Let not against thy spouse thine anger rise!
O versed in every turn of human art,
Forgive the weakness of a woman's heart!
The righteous powers that mortal lots dispose
Decree us to sustain a length of woes,   220
And from the flower of life the bliss deny
To bloom together, fade away, and die.
O let me, let me not thine anger move,
That I forbore, thus, thus, to speak my love;
Thus in fond kisses, while the transport warms,   225
Pour out my soul, and die within thy arms!
I dreaded fraud! Men, faithless men, betray
Our easy faith, and make the sex their prey.
Against the fondness of my heart I strove,
'Twas caution, O my lord, not want of love!   230
Like me had Helen feared, with wanton charms
Ere the fair mischief set two worlds in arms,
Ere Greece rose dreadful in th' avenging day,
Thus had she feared, she had not gone astray.
But heaven, averse to Greece, in wrath decreed   235
That she should wander, and that Greece should bleed;
Blind to the ills that from injustice flow,
She coloured all our wretched lives with woe.
But why these sorrows, when my lord arrives?
I yield, I yield! My own Ulysses lives!   240
The secrets of the bridal bed are known
To thee, to me, to Actoris alone
(My father's present in the spousal hour,
The sole attendant on our genial bower).
Since what no eye has seen thy tongue revealed,   245
Hard and distrustful as I am, I yield.'
          Touched to the soul, the king with rapture hears,
Hangs round her neck, and speaks his joy in tears.
As to the shipwrecked mariner, the shores
Delightful rise, when angry Neptune roars;   250
Then, when the surge in thunder mounts the sky,
And gulfed in crowds, at once the sailors die,
If one more happy, while the tempest raves,
Outlives the tumult of conflicting waves,
All pale, with ooze deformed, he views the strand,   255

And plunging forth with transport grasps the land:
The ravished queen with equal rapture glows,
Clasps her loved lord, and to his bosom grows.

Ulysses is re-united with his father, Laertes. The relatives of the suitors attempt revenge, but Ulysses defeats them, and peace is finally restored in Ithaca.

Notes

Iliad

from **Book 1** **2 heavenly goddess**: Homer's Muse. **8 doom**: judgement. **195 interest**: self-interest. **197 generous**: noble. **202 coursers**: horses. **214 Due to**: Owing to me because of. **227 want not**: is no lack of. **241 dame**: maiden. **242 bark**: ship. **255 That**: i.e. his wrath. **257 This**: i.e. reason. **262 the sister ... of Jove**: Juno. **265 confessed**: disclosed. **266 sable**: black. **273 progeny**: offspring. **277 awful**: awe-inspiring. **295 boiling**: turbulent with passion. **300 horrid**: dreadful. **307 generous**: abundant. **309 sceptre**: (the symbol of power and justice). **316 Tremendous**: Awe-inspiring. **inviolate to**: unable to be broken by. **320 purpled**: blood-stained. **322 deplore**: lament. **328 again**: in return. **702 cares**: concerns. **706 Involved**: Wrapped. **719 silver-footed queen**: Thetis. **721 signal**: Jove's thunder, indicating his accession to Thetis' request. **729 Anxious**: Creative of anxiety. **746 sire**: father. **780 awful**: awe-inspiring.

from **Book 2** **258 busy**: active. **259 studious to defame**: intent on attacking people's good reputations. **269 still**: always. **289 generous**: of high-born women. **298 prize**: Briseis. **303 the king of kings**: Agamemnon. **309 asperse**: defame. **328 bunch**: hump. **539 splendour**: brightness. **544 course**: fly. **550 meads**: meadows. **564 king of kings**: Agamemnon. **569 mien**: bearing.

from **Book 3** **172 fatal**: (i) fated (ii) producing fatal effect. **176 dreadful**: awe-inspiring. **179 Sparta's king**: Menelaus. **180 beamy**: massive. **184 Her husband's love**: love for Menelaus. **200 narrative**: garrulous. **301 wanting**: lacking. **493 still**: always. **495 main**: sea. **526 officious**: attentive. **534 fame**: bad reputation.

from **Book 4** **501 purple**: blood-stained. **504 horrid**: causing horror. **511 darts**: arrows, javelins. **512 promiscuous**: mingled. **516 rills**: streams. **519 main**: sea.

from **Book 5** **611 swain**: countryman. **612 clear**: winnow. **616 hinds**: farm workers.

from **Book 6** **491 the mourner**: Andromache. **497 his only hope**: Astyanax. **520 tenor**: course. **529 decent**: in a fitting manner.

537 hapless: unlucky. **555 the vengeful Spartan**: Menelaus. **564 Attaint**: Defame. **574 presage**: presentiment. **576 hoary**: white. **591 clay**: earth (forming a tomb). **603 preferred**: offered. **604 ethereal**: heavenly. **611 reeking**: steaming with blood. **626 doom**: time fated for his death. **644 deplored**: lamented.

from **Book 8**   **687 refulgent**: gleaming with reflected light. **688 azure**: blue. **693 verdure**: greenness. **695 in prospect**: displayed to view. **706 umbered**: darkened with battle-stains. **707 coursers**: horses.

from **Book 9**   **427 care**: offspring. **432 on the main**: on islands near Troy. **443 My spouse**: Briseis. **461 profound**: deep. **463 Priam's single son**: Hector. **466 verge**: boundary. **485 braves**: defies. **489 commerce**: negotiations. **542 asserts**: champions. **634 Sire**: Jove. **642 the haughty king**: Agamemnon. **643 Nor**: Neither.

from **Book 12**   **380 vindicate**: justify. **396 Or**: Either.

from **Book 13**   **187 terrible**: terrifying. **199 proved**: tested.

from **Book 14**   **196 valves**: hinges. **200 aërial**: airy. **208 laboured**: carefully executed. **210 zone**: girdle. **359 prove**: experience. **361 pressed**: slept with. **dame**: wife. **365 either Theban dame**: Semele and Alcmena. **367 Phoenix' daughter**: Europa. **377 familiar**: (i) well known (ii) of members of our family. **379 review**: look upon again. **384 genial**: procreative.

from **Book 15**   **410 fosse**: rampart. **411 cars**: chariots. **729 involves**: encloses. **734 splendour**: brightness. **744 phalanx**: battle-formation. **moveless as**: as immovable as. **752 impends**: overhangs. **755 shroud**: sail. **763 expatiate**: spread out. **ranker**: more luxuriant in grass.

from **Book 16**   **193 terrific**: terrifying. **202 Like**: Similarly. **203 view**: appearance. **540 goddess … eyes**: Juno. **548 partial**: biased. **948 press**: thick of the fight. **959 champain**: plain. **964 dooms**: fates. **967 baldric**: cross-belt. **968 corselet**: breastplate. **969 nerve**: muscle. **970 Stupid**: Stunned. **974 manage**: training. **981 protended**: stuck out. **982 herded in**: sought security in. **985 social train**: group of comrades. **1000 effused**: poured out. **1002 He**: Hector. **1005 fancied**: imagined. **1015 sped**: prospered (ironical). **1016 Supine**: Lying on his back.

from **Book 18**   **161 sanguine**: bloody. **242 aegis**: protection. **253 splendours**: shafts of light. **639 swarths**: cornfields. **644 gripe**: grab. **656 pales**: bands.

from **Book 19** 378 **train:** army. 392 **father of the fire:** Vulcan. 398 **cuishes:** leg armour. 403 **athwart:** across. 414 **honours:** adornments. 419 **pinion:** wing. 423 **sire:** master. 424 **only:** alone. 428 **traces:** straps. 436 **ethereal:** heavenly. 446 **generous:** well-bred. 447 **sensible of:** sensitive to. 448 **wain:** chariot. 451 **portentous:** foretelling the future. 453 **files:** military columns. 458 **The bright . . . god:** Apollo. 459 **Confessed:** Revealed. 467 **prodigies:** omens.

from **Book 21** 43 **late:** recently. 50 **reign:** kingdom. 52 **that god:** Jove or Fate. 106 **kind:** family. 115 **What boots . . . deplore:** What use is lamentation. 136 **corse:** corpse. 145 **immolated:** sacrificed. 269 **stay:** stop. 292 **pregnant:** fruitful. 298 **mazy:** winding.

from **Book 22** 139 **ungenerous:** ignoble. 142 **timely followed:** if they had been immediately implemented. 148 **charge:** blame. 151 **my country's terror:** Achilles. 174 **dreadful:** awe-inspiring. 177 **splendours:** brilliant shafts of light. 189 **foreright:** directly forward. 193 **umbrage:** shade. 207 **vulgar:** ordinary. 390 **all collected:** summoning all his courage. 391 **Jove's bold bird:** the eagle. 392 **truss:** seize in its claws. 395 **cone:** conical helmet. 427 **prevalence:** power. 429 **sepulture:** burial. 441 **the weeping dame:** Hecuba. 495 **fell:** ruthless. 497 **nervous:** sinewy.

from **Book 23** 92 **irremeable:** admitting of no return.

from **Book 24** 618 **one:** Hector. 671 **sincere:** pure. 672 **cordial:** comforting. **dashed:** mixed. 675 **goddess:** Thetis. 698 **obsequies:** funeral rites. 926 **pressed the plain:** fell in battle.

Odyssey

from **Book 1** 5 **clime:** country. 6 **manners:** modes of life. 8 **natal:** home. 10 **herds:** the Oxen of the Sun.

from **Book 2** 97 **defame:** attack the good name of. 110 **ornaments of death:** funeral shroud. 120 **conscious:** complicit.

from **Book 5** 72 **grot:** cave. 80 **Without:** Outside. **sylvan:** wooded. 86 **loquacious:** noisy. 87 **And:** Both. 88 **Depending:** Hanging. 91 **several:** separate. 93 **virid:** verdant. 264 **yet:** still. 270 **august:** stately, dignified.

from **Book 6** 96 **sounding:** echoing. 99 **cisterns:** pools. 104 **herbage:** grass. 105 **emulous:** each trying to outdo her fellows. **lave:** wash. 108 **strand:** beach. 122 **bay:** pursue. 123 **lawn:** meadow. 134 **various:**

thrown in different directions. **erroneous**: in the wrong direction.
136 redoubles: re-echoes.   **145 dryads**: wood-nymphs.   **146 azure ...**
flood: sea-nymphs.   **148 invades**: intrudes on my hearing.   **149 umbra-**
geous: shady.   **151 cincture**: circle of foliage.   **154 rude**: rough.
157 elate: exultant.   **160 dissipates**: scatters.   **164 deforms**: makes
ugly.   **169 dubious**: hesitating.   **174 accosts**: addresses.   **188 swim**:
glide.   **203 Awed from access**: Afraid to come near.   **209 Inured**:
Hardened.   **215 vest**: tunic.

from **Book 7**   **146 mould**: soil.   **151 verdant**: green.   **164 descried**:
seen.   **165 discoloured**: i.e. ripened.

from **Book 8**   **492 unguents**: ointments.   **506 writhen**: fashioned by
twisting.

from **Book 9**   **288 cares**: tasks.   **297 discovered**: revealed.   **349 Nor**:
Neither.   **352 maw**: stomach.   **445 inspire**: stir up.   **458 wimble**:
brace.   **476 rifted rocks**: rocks split by chasms.   **482 or ... or**: either ...
or.   **505 purple**: clothing (i.e. wool).   **506 fleecy care**: flocks which were
their shepherd's responsibility.   **514 implicit**: entwined.   **confide**:
trust.   **524 Charged**: Loaded.   **526 lag**: last.

from **Book 10**   **242 brindled**: streaked.   **244 blandishment**: affectionate
gestures.   **283 mast**: fruit of trees, used as pig food.   **284 fruits of cornel**:
cornel-cherries.   **285 unsavoury**: disgusting.   **378 mantled**:
frothed.   **384 falchion**: curved sword.   **402 accents**: types of
speech.   **412 genial**: marriage.   **417 carpets**: drapes.   **418 against the**
view: to the sight.   **421 dulcet**: sweet.   **433 ewer**: pitcher.   **436 laver**:
basin.   **439 Viands**: Food, meats.   **447 cates**: food.   **458 virtue**:
power.   **462 dishonest**: hideous.   **473 adamantine**: impenetrably hard.

from **Book 11**   **235 honours**: leaves.   **584 wan**: pallid.   **588 the**
Theban: Tiresias.

from **Book 12**   **208 ductile**: malleable.   **212 strain**: song.   **219 descries**:
spots.   **223 lay**: song.

from **Book 13**   **121 hawsers**: anchor-cables.   **143 measured back**:
journeyed back over.   **334 refined**: skilled.

from **Book 14**   **12 pile**: building.   **15 pales**: stakes.   **17 Frequent**: Close
together.   **26 buskins**: boots.   **28 on the rural care**: looking after their
herds.   **83 succinct**: tied up.   **91 Broachers**: Spits.

from **Book 16**   **202 laboured**: carefully-worked.   **220 weeds obscene**:
filthy clothes.   **228 frame**: body.   **236 social**: shared (with his son).

from **Book 17**   **355 mazy**: swerving.   **leveret**: young hare.   **359 reptiles**:

creeping creatures. 363 **Salute**: Greet. 385 **wind**: smell. **tainted**: imbued with animal scent. 387 **unnerve**: weaken. 388 **bare**: needy.

from **Book 19** 548 **redound**: flow. 561 **pest**: destruction. 578 **immured**: walled round. 581 **blazon**: tell of. **menial fair**: servant girls. 582 **devote**: damn.

from **Book 21** 442 **strain**: tune. 443 **vocal wire**: string. 444 **strains**: tightens. 447 **essayed**: tried.

from **Book 22** 4 **quivered deaths**: arrows. 24 **spurned**: kicked over. 29 **haggard**: terrified.

from **Book 23** 160 **fusile**: melted. 161 **his**: Ulysses'. 181 **translate**: move. 182 **Framed**: Made. 197 **conjoins**: was added to it. 200 **bole**: trunk. 206 **elephant**: ivory. 207 **ungoverned**: undisciplined. 214 **strained**: embraced. 243 **spousal hour**: wedding day. 255 **ooze**: muddy water. **deformed**: made unsightly. 258 **grows**: clings tight.

Glossary of Names and Places

ACHAIA, Greece.

ACHILLES, son of Peleus and the sea-nymph Thetis; the bravest and most passionate of the Greek warriors at Troy.

ACTORIS, a female servant of Penelope.

AEOLUS, a mortal to whom Jove gave control of the winds; Ulysses was received hospitably by him and was given a bag containing the adverse winds; these were, however, released (with disastrous consequences) by Ulysses' men.

AËTION: see ANDROMACHE.

AGAMEMNON, King of Argos; leader of the Greek army at Troy and brother of Menelaus.

AJAX (AIAS), brawniest of the Greek warriors at Troy; called 'the greater Ajax' to differentiate him from 'the lesser Ajax', captain of the Locrian contingent in the Greek army.

ALCIDES = Hercules: see ALCMENA.

ALCIMUS, a Thessalian warrior.

ALCINOÜS, King of the Phaeacians.

ALCMENA, wife of Amphitryon; seduced by Jove: Hercules was the product of their union; Juno's jealousy made her Hercules' lifelong enemy.

ALTES, king of the Leleges and father of Laothoë, the mother (by Priam) of Lycaon.

ANDROMACHE, wife of Hector and mother of Astyanax; daughter of Aëtion, King of Thebes in Cilicia; her father and brothers were killed by Achilles, her mother taken prisoner and subsequently ransomed.

ANTICLEA, mother of Ulysses.

ANTINOÜS, the most vocal and arrogant of Penelope's suitors.

APOLLO, god of the sun and music; pro-Trojan; his principal shrine on Delos.

ARGIVE, from Argos.

ARISBÈ: see Eëtion.

ASIUS, a plain near the river Caÿster in Asia Minor.

ASTYANAX, the young son of Hector and Andromache.

ATÈ, the personification of blind folly.

ATREUS' SON = Agamemnon.

ATRIDES = Agamemnon, or Menelaus (both sons of Atreus).

AURORA (EOS), the goddess of dawn, who fell in love with the hunter-giant Orion; Diana became jealous and killed him.

AUTOMEDON, charioteer to Achilles.

BACCHUS (DIONYSUS): see SEMELE.

BALIUS, one of Achilles' horses.

BOREAS, the North Wind.

BRISEIS, Achilles' captive maiden, seized by Agamemnon.

CADMUS: see LEUCOTHEA.

CALYPSO, a nymph who lived on the island of Ogygia, where she kept Ulysses for seven years.

CASTOR AND POLLUX (POLYDEUCES), twin sons of Leda, and brothers to Helen; assumed by Homer to have died before the Trojan War.

CAŸSTER: see ASIUS.

CERES (DEMETER), goddess of corn and agriculture; mother of Proserpina and Jason by Jove; her lover Iäsion was killed by Jove in jealousy.

CHARYBDIS: see SCYLLA.

CHIRON: see PELION.

CICONES, a people of Thrace, raided by Ulysses and his crew.

CILICIAN: see ANDROMACHE.

CIMMERIANS, a legendary people living at the edge of the world; from their dark, misty land, Ulysses gains access to the spirits of the dead.

CIRCE, an enchantress-goddess, living on the island of Aeaea.

CRANAË, an island visited by Paris en route from Sparta to Troy.

CYCLOPES, a race of one-eyed giants, visited by Ulysses and his crew.

DANAË, a princess of Argos, seduced by Jove in a shower of gold; Perseus, slayer of Medusa, was the product of their union.

DARDAN(IAN) = Trojan.

DELOS: see APOLLO.

DIAN(A) (ARTEMIS), goddess of chastity and the chase.

DIOMEDES, leader of the contingent from Argos and Tiryns in the Greek army at Troy.

EËTION, King of Imbrus, an ally of Priam; he purchased Lycaon from Eunaeus, and despatched him to Arisbè near Troy, whence Lycaon could easily get back to his native city.

ERYMANTH(US), a mountain, river and town in Arcadia.

ERYNNYS, a malignant Fury, the provoker of outrageous deeds.

EUMAEUS, Ithacan swineherd; loyal to his master Ulysses.

EUNAEUS: see JASON and LYCAON.

EUROPA, daughter of Agenor, King of Tyre; seduced by Jove in the form of a bull; she bore Minos and Rhadamanthus as the result of the union.

EURYCLEA, Ulysses' nurse.

EURYLOCHUS, companion of Ulysses; prudent in his dealings with Circe, but reckless in his participation in the slaughter of the Oxen of the Sun.

GLAUCUS, Lycian warrior; the friend of Sarpedon.

HECTOR, son of Priam, husband of Andromache, and father of Astyanax; the bravest of the Trojan warriors, with a strongly-developed sense of responsibility to his city.

HECUBA, Queen of Troy; wife of Priam.

HELEN, daughter of Jove by the mortal Leda; formerly wife of Menelaus; a woman of goddess-like beauty; her abduction to Troy by Paris (to whom she had been promised by Venus, as the result of his award of the prize to her in a contest between the goddesses) caused the Trojan War.

HELLESPONT, narrow straits between the Aegean Sea and the Sea of Marmora.

HERCULES (HERACLES), the mightiest of the legendary Greek heroes.

HERMES, the herald of the gods.

HESPER, the Evening Star.

HIPPOPLACUS, mountain overlooking Thebes, home of Andromache.

HYPERIA, a spring at Argos.

IÄSON: see CERES.

IDA, mountain near Troy, from which Jove viewed the war.

ILION = Troy.

IRIS, goddess of the rainbow and messenger of the gods.

IXION, husband of Dia, whom Jove seduced; Perithous, the friend of Theseus, was the result of their union.

JASON, mythic hero, the leader of the Argonauts; his son was Eunaeus, King of Lemnos.

JOVE (ZEUS), father and most powerful of the gods; married to his sister Juno.

JUNO (HERA), wife and sister of Jove; vehemently anti-Trojan.

LAERTES, father of Ulysses.

LAESTRYGONIANS, a race of cannibal giants, visited by Ulysses and his men.

LAODICÈ, eldest daughter of Priam and Hecuba.

LAOTHOË, daughter of Altes, king of the Leleges, and mother of Lycaon.

LATONA (LETO), goddess seduced by Jove; their offspring were Apollo and Diana.

LELEGIA, the dominion of the Leleges, encompassing various cities in mainland Greece, the islands, and Asia Minor.

LEMNOS: see JASON.

LESBOS, a Greek island off the coast of Asia Minor.

LEUCOTHEA, formerly Ino, one of the four daughters of Cadmus, but transformed into a sea-deity.

LINUS, the supposed subject of an ancient Greek song of lament; according to one version, a music teacher, killed with his own lyre by Hercules.

LOTOPHAGI, a mythic people visited by Ulysses; they lived on the lotus-fruit which made them blissfully oblivious of their homeland.

LYCAON, son of Priam and Laothoë; captured by Achilles and sold as a slave to Eunaeus, King of Lemnos; purchased by Eëtion, King of Imbrus, who facilitated his return to Troy; soon afterwards killed by Achilles.

LYCIAN: see SARPEDON.

LYRNESSIAN SLAVE = Briseis (captured by Achilles at the siege of Lyrnessus).

MARS (ARES), god of war; pro-Trojan.

MENELAUS, King of Sparta, brother of Agamemnon, and husband of Helen.

MENTOR, one of Ulysses' most faithful friends; left in charge of Ulysses' domestic affairs in his absence; Minerva assumes his form (*Odyssey*, Book 2).

MINERVA (ATHENE), the blue-eyed goddess of wisdom and war; Jove's daughter; hostile to the Trojans, because slighted by the Judgement of Paris.

MINOS: see EUROPA.

MUSES, goddesses of the poetry and the other arts.

MYCENE, daughter of Inachus.

MYRMIDONS, Achilles' troops; their race was said to have been transformed from ants.

NAUSICAA, Phaeacian princess; daughter of Alcinoüs and Aretè.

NEPTUNE (POSEIDON), god of the sea; pro-Greek, but turns against Ulysses after the blinding of his son, the Cyclops Polyphemus.

NEREIDS, sea-nymphs.

NESTOR, King of Pylos; the oldest of the Greek warriors at Troy; garrulous, but wise; the father of Antilochus.

OLYMPUS, mountain home of the gods (in northern Greece).

ORION: see AURORA.

ORTYGIA, Delos, where Diana destroyed Orion (see AURORA).

OXEN OF THE SUN, cattle kept by Apollo on the island of Thrinacia, and killed (despite Tiresias' warning) by Ulysses' men, with disastrous consequences.

PALLAS = Minerva.

PAPHIAN QUEEN = Venus (born on Paphos).

PARIS, son of Priam and Hecuba; called upon to settle a dispute between Juno, Minerva, and Venus as to which was the most beautiful, he chose Venus, and, as a reward, was promised Helen, whom he abducted from her home in Sparta, thus causing the Trojan War.

PATROCLUS, friend of Achilles, with whom he had been brought up.

PEDASUS, a Lelegian city, under the dominion of Altes.

PELEUS, father of Achilles.

PELIAN JAVELIN, Achilles' spear (which only he could wield), fashioned from wood felled on Mt Pelion.

PELIDES = Achilles (son of Peleus).

PELION, woody mountain in Thessaly, where Achilles was educated by the centaur Chiron.

PENELOPE, faithful wife of Ulysses, beleaguered in his absence by suitors.

PERITHOUS: see IXION.

PERSEUS: see DANAË.

PHAEACIA, island kingdom of Alcinoüs and Aretè, where Ulysses is cast ashore.

PHOEBUS = Apollo.

PHOENIX, a Thessalian prince to whom the charge of the young Achilles was entrusted by Peleus.

PHORCYS, a sea god, the son of Nereus.

PHRYGIAN = Trojan.

PLUTO (HADES), King of the Underworld.

PODARGE, one of the Harpies, the mother of Xanthus and Balius, Achilles' horses.

POLYDAMAS, a friend of Hector who (in *Iliad* Book 18) counsels the Trojans to withdraw within the city, to avoid the danger of Achilles' attack.

POLYDORE, youngest son of Priam, by Laothoë; killed by Achilles (*Iliad*, Book 21).

POLYPHEMUS, a Cyclops, the son of Poseidon.

PRAMNIAN, a type of wine produced in Thrace.

PRIAM, the aged King of Troy; father of fifty sons, including Paris and Hector; husband of Hecuba.

PTHIA, the birthplace of Achilles in Thessaly.

RHADAMANTH: see EUROPA.

SARPEDON, son of Jove and leader of Priam's auxiliaries from Lycia in Asia Minor.

SATURNIUS = Jove (son of Saturn).

SCAEAN GATE, one of the gates of Troy.

SCAMANDER, a river on the plain of Troy.

SCYLLA, a monster living in a cave, with the whirlpool of Charybdis opposite.

SEMELE, daughter of Cadmus, King of Thebes; made pregnant by Jove with Bacchus.

SINTIANS, inhabitants of Lesbos, who rescued Vulcan, when he was thrown out of heaven by Jove for taking Juno's part in a quarrel with her husband.

SIRENS, temptresses who lure sailors to destruction by their songs; Ulysses steels himself against their seductions by pressing wax in his ears and having himself lashed to the mast of his ship.

STYGIAN SHORE, the banks of the Styx, the river of the Underworld.

TÄYGETUS, a mountain of Laconia.

TELEMACHUS, son of Ulysses.

THEBÈ: see ANDROMACHE.

THERSITES, the only low-born leader among the Greeks; hump-backed, ugly, disaffected, and abusive.

THESSALIA: see PTHIA.

THETIS: see ACHILLES. Thetis had been loved by Jove before her marriage to Peleus.

THUNDERER = Jove.

TIRESIAS, the blind Theban seer, consulted by Ulysses about his return to Ithaca.

TYDIDES = Diomedes (son of Tydeus).

TYRO, a beautiful nymph, daughter of Salmoneus, King of Elis.

ULYSSES (ODYSSEUS), King of Ithaca; the cleverest of the Greek heroes; artful and diplomatic; having played a crucial part in the fall of Troy (including the invention of the Wooden Horse), he wanders the Mediterranean for ten years before arriving home.

VENUS (APHRODITE), goddess of love; her promise of Helen to Paris brought about the Trojan War.

VULCAN (HEPHAESTUS), lame god of fire; son of Juno; blacksmith to the gods, and builder of the gods' houses on Olympus; pro-Greek in the Trojan War.

XANTHUS, (i) a river of Troy, (ii) one of Achilles' horses.